GREAT LAKES COLLISIONS, WRECKS & DISASTERS

SHIPS 400 TO 998 FEET

WAYNE LOUIS KADAR

Avery Color Studios, Inc.
Gwinn, Michigan

©2008 Avery Color Studios, Inc.

ISBN-13: 978-1-892384-47-8
ISBN-10: 1-892384-47-7

Library of Congress Control Number: 2007943890

First Edition 2008
10   9   8   7   6   5   4   3   2   1

Published by
Avery Color Studios, Inc.
Gwinn, Michigan 49841

Cover photos: the *M/V Montrose* grounded beneath the Ambassador Bridge, from the collections of the State of Michigan Archives; the *George M. Humphrey,* from the collection of the Door County Maritime Museum; the *J.P. Morgan, Jr.,* from the collection of the Bayliss Library, Sault Ste. Marie, Michigan; the Grosse Ile Toll Bridge after the *John T. Hutchinson* smashed into it, photo from the Grosse Ile Michigan Historical Society.

To Karen

TABLE OF CONTENTS

INTRODUCTION

Through the pages of this book, the incidents involving the largest of the Great Lakes ships will be presented. It's hard to comprehend the size of a Great Lakes freighter until you see one up close. They are huge!

The ships are so large one questions how they could fall victim to the lakes. How could mere waves break apart a ship made of steel? How could these mammoths of the lakes not avoid each other yet there have been many collisions? How can a huge Great Lakes freighter run aground when there is so much deep water.

The huge size of the Great Lakes freighter Carl D. Bradley *can be appreciated compared to the people lining the lock walls at Sault Ste. Marie. From the State of Michigan Archives.*

Unless the reader has had the opportunity to get close to a freighter the full impact of the size of these vessels cannot be understood. In an effort to help the reader comprehend how huge these ships are each vessel in this book will be compared to an item with which most people are familiar.

Semi-truck tractors and trailers are about 55-feet long. In some states the law allows longer units and in some shorter but 55-feet seems to be the standard. To help the reader understand how large a ship is each vessel in the book will be compared to semi-trucks and trailers lined up end to end.

As an example of the method used to compare a ship to semi-trucks and trailers the following is a comparison of trucks and trailers to probably the most famous of the Great Lakes freighter shipwrecks, the legendary *Edmund Fitzgerald*.

Edmund Fitzgerald   729 Feet in Length

The "Big Fitz" as it was affectionately called, was the largest ship on the lakes when she was launched. At 729-feet she was the length of over 13 semi-trucks and trailers parked end to end.

Hopefully this comparison will provide the reader an image to visualize the sheer size of these mammoths of the lakes.

All avid freighter watchers need to someday make a pilgrimage to a location where they can get so close to a freighter that they can feel the rumble of the engine as a Great Lakes freighter passes by. There are several places around the lakes where freighter watchers have an opportunity to get close to these steel mammoths.

The Welland Canal, separating Lakes Ontario and Erie, offers a 25-mile long opportunity to watch ships pass though locks and under lift bridges. Many people recommend the breakwall at Duluth, Minnesota for a close viewing opportunity while others claim the Detroit River, between Lake Erie and Lake St. Clair, where ships pass in the narrow waterway providing a great view of the freighters. No list of great places to get a close up view of a freighter would be complete without including the Soo Locks. At both Sault Ste. Marie, Ontario and Sault Ste. Marie, Michigan, Great Lake ships and their foreign counterparts pass through the locks that raise or lower them 21-feet while freighter lovers have the opportunity to watch from viewing platforms.

The author's favorite place to get close up to the ships plying the Great Lakes is Vantage Point in Port Huron, Michigan. Vantage Point is located on the St. Clair River where all boat traffic moving between the upper lakes of Michigan, Superior and Huron and the lower lakes of Erie and Ontario must pass. The Vantage Point is a building with a wall of windows facing the river with inside and outside seating. The building offers meeting areas, a free Great Lakes book library, free use of binoculars, free lectures on Great Lake topics, a lunch

The size of the ship can be seen compared to the men standing on the dock. From Hugh Clark Great Lakes Photographic collection.

counter and a narrated history and statistics of each ship as it passes. As a bonus the headquarters of Boatnerd.com is located there.

The reason lovers of the lakes and the ships that travel on them need to get close to a Great Lakes freighter is to appreciate their immense size. They are huge!

Note: Some sections of this book have appeared in previous books by the author. They have been included because they are pertinent to a book devoted to Great Lakes Freighter Accidents and Disasters.

SHIPS AT LEAST 400 FEET
WILLIAM C. WARREN

In February 1948, a drunken party was held on a beach on Lake Huron. The estimated three thousand merry makers gathered at Black Point, northwest of the Presque Isle lighthouse. The location was the site where the Canadian steamer *William C. Warren* had grounded in shallow water two months earlier.

Neal Curtis, a local Conservation Officer who observed the intoxicated bunch said, "It is the worst case of... intoxication he had ever witnessed." They came for the free meal that was said to be there but many became so inebriated the party goers staggered around the beach and interfered with the men who were attempting to salvage the cargo of the *Warren*.

The *William C. Warren*, a 400-foot Canadian grain carrier, was southbound on the lake during a horrendous blow. The ship, loaded with 80,000 bushels of wheat, struggled against the gale force winds and mounting seas. Captain Mac Beth set a course for North Bay about 20 miles north of Alpena and about 18 miles east southeast of Rogers City. The bay would offer a refuge

William C. Warren   400 Feet in Length

5

The William C. Warren *ashore after the storm. The photo shows a crew member being transported on the Breeches Buoy. From the William D. Lewis collection.*

from the ravages of the stormy lake. Unfortunately, the course took them dangerously close to the rocky shoals of Black Point.

The *William C. Warren* ground to a halt in the shoal water of Black Point riding up high on the rocky bottom. The waves crashed over the stranded steamer and washed the decks with torrents of water.

When attempts of the *Warren* to free herself from the rocks failed, the captain made a call to Tom Reid's Great Lakes Towing Company in Sarnia, Ontario for assistance. The wrecking tug Favorite and a barge were brought along side the crippled steamer and some cargo was removed to lighten the vessel but when the *Warren's* engines roared and belched black smoke into the cold November sky the ship still would not budge. Finally a line was run from the tug Favorite. The tug drew up the slack from the line and the captain called for full power as the tug churned up the water into white foam. Again the *Warren* did not move. Further attempts by the tug were not successful and the Canadian steamer remained on the rocks.

After it was found that the ship probably could not be removed from the rocky bottom, the owners of the *Warren*, Upton-St. Lawrence Transportation Company, and its insurance underwriter determined the ship to be a total loss. The insurance underwriter paid out to the owners, and the hulk remained on the rocks.

Tom Reid, owner of the Great Lakes Towing Company, purchased the rights to salvage the *William C. Warren* from the insurance underwriters for the sum of $5,000. With his expertise he was sure the ship could be removed from its resting place. In April of 1948 he returned to Black Point and worked to free the *Warren* from the rocky bottom. With much effort the *Warren* was removed from the shoal water and the leaking, crippled vessel was towed to a dry dock in Collingwood, Ontario.

The ship was repaired and put back into service. Since then, the *William C. Warren* has earned well over its estimat-

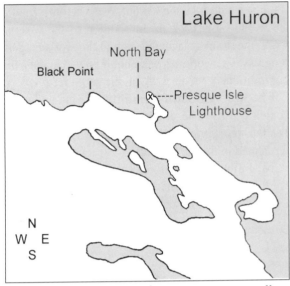

ed value of a half of a million dollars. The $5,000 was an excellent investment on the part of Tom Reid.

Prior to the *Warren* being removed from the rocks of Black Point, the cargo was sold to two local men, Alfred Erkfitz of Rogers City and Moore Combs of Hillman. They rigged a pipeline from shore, 800-feet out into the lake to the ill-fated ship. The cargo of wheat was then pumped to shore. But, the salvage attempt was fraught with problems. An early winter caused ice to form at the wreck site hampering their efforts. If the wind blew in from the

The William C. Warren *aground and frozen in place in North Bay. The photograph shows work being done to salvage her cargo. From the William D. Lewis Collection.*

south it would take the ice out, but when the wind came from the north the ice would blow back in. In addition to the weather inhibiting the salvage work, the drunks staggered around the workers, getting in their way slowed progress. The workmen were not involved in the public display of alcoholism but it did hinder their work on the cargo recovery.

The free meal lured them in, many ate and some became so drunk they couldn't... fly. The drunks at the site of the wrecked steamer *William C. Warren* were... ducks. They ate the wheat cargo which had become wet and fermented in the cargo holds.

Neal Curtis, a local conservation officer said. "It's the worst case of wildlife intoxication he has ever witnessed. They would get so drunk they would just flop and stagger around."

SHIPS AT LEAST 400 FEET

JAMES GAYLEY

Throughout this book If there is one common thread connecting the vessels involved in a collision with another ship, it would have to be fog.

Before there was radar, ships caught in fog could only slow down, sound their fog signal, post a lookout, and pray they would not run into or be run into by another ship. In the morning of August 7, 1912, two large steel steamers met in a dense fog covering most of Lake Superior.

The Pittsburg Steamship Company's 454-foot steel ship the Rensselaer, had taken on a load of iron ore and was heading across Lake Superior to the locks at Sault Ste. Marie. The twelve-year-old ship was in the open water when a layer of fog formed over the lake reducing visibility.

Lookouts were posted at the bow and near the bridge to watch and listen for signs of other ships as the ship continued on her easterly course.

Also on the lake on that morning was the steamer *James Gayley*. The ten-year-old, 416-foot long *Gayley* was owned by the Mitchell and Company.

With a crew of 27 and four female passengers, the *Gayley* was crossing the length of Lake Superior with a load of coal bound for Duluth, Minnesota on the western end of the lake.

James Gayley 416 Feet in Length

The James Gayley. *From the collections of the Port Huron Museum.*

Traveling west and slightly north from the Soo Locks, the *Gayley* was on a course which would take it over the tip of the Michigan's Keweenaw Peninsula, a rocky peninsula which extends almost 70 miles from the lake's southern shore.

The Rensselaer had been traveling northeast to clear the peninsula and then made a course change to the southeast towards the locks. The ship would then travel the length of Lake Huron, Lake St. Clair, down the Detroit River into Lake Erie and on to Cleveland.

The *Gayley* was about 35 miles east of the peninsula slowly picking its way through the thick fog and rain when the steel bow of the Rensselaer appeared off its starboard bow. Captain Stewart ran from the bridge to wake the passengers in the starboard side staterooms. Wearing only their night-clothes, the women made it to the deck just as the Rensselaer smashed into the foreword starboard side of the *Gayley*. The women's stateroom was demolished. They would surely have been killed had they stayed in the room.

The crew of the Rensselaer quickly put the axe to the tow line to the *Corliss*, the barge she was pulling. In case the Rensselaer should sink they didn't want to pull the *Corliss* to the bottom with her.

The Rensselaer rebounded back from the *Gayley*. Seeing the other ship listing badly, the captain of the Rensselaer directed his ship to the side of the *Gayley*. The passengers were helped off the *Gayley* onto the deck of the Rensselaer. The ships separated before any of the others could jump, but the Rensselaer was again maneuvered next to the sinking ship and nineteen more crew made it off the *Gayley*.

The other members of the crew lowered a lifeboat and escaped the *Gayley*, as the ship slipped below the waves and sunk to the depths of Lake Superior just 16 minutes after the collision.

The Rensselaer with the crew and passengers of the *Gayley* began to steam towards Marquette, Michigan over 100 miles away. With a large gaping hole in her bow, the Rensselaer appeared to be settling. Fearing his ship was sinking, the captain ordered the emergency whistle to be sounded in hopes to attract other nearby boats.

After an hour, the downbound steamer *Strathcona*, maneuvered close to the Rensselaer and the crew and passengers of the *Gayley* again were transferred to another ship.

The Rensselaer continued on her race to port. Despite the severe damage to her bow, the bulkheads held and the ship made it safely to Marquette.

The *Strathcona* with the crew and passengers of the *Gayley* crept through the fog to the Sault locks. There they disembarked to await further instructions from the company.

The barge *Corliss* picked up the four *Gayley* crew who escaped the sinking ship by a lifeboat and the barge was found by another passing ship and was towed to port.

The Rensselaer received $10,000 in damage (in 1912 dollars) but was repaired and put back into service. Her career lasted another 35 years when she was towed to the scrap yard.

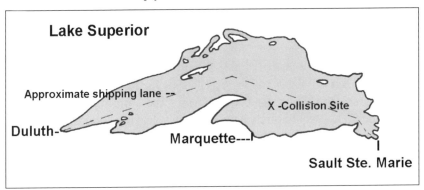

Lake Superior

Approximate shipping lane --

X -Collision Site

Duluth-

Marquette---

Sault Ste. Marie

Just ten years after the 416-foot *James Gayley* was launched she met with disaster in the middle of the lake. The once proud ship now lies under hundreds of feet of cold Lake Superior water, probably never to be seen again. It was a disaster, but due to the quick thinking and heroic actions of both captains there were no fatalities. Everyone made it safely back to shore.

SHIPS AT LEAST 400 FEET
CYPRUS

Protocol of the Life Saving Service required stations on the Great Lakes to constantly observe the lakes. During daylight hours surfmen kept vigilance of the lake from a lookout tower; at night surfmen walked along the shore keeping a watch for lake vessels showing signs of distress.

The patrolman carried with them several pieces of equipment including a lantern and a metal check. The checks were small pieces of metal with the name of the station and the crewmember's number stamped on it. In locations where there were adjoining Life Saving Stations, the beach patrolman would walk to a location where he would meet a patrolman from the adjoining station. They would exchange the checks and take it back to the station proving that they had indeed walked the full distance between the stations.

If there were no adjoining stations, the patrolman carried a patrol clock, or punch clock. He would walk to the end of his patrol area where a key was hung on a post. The key was inserted into the clock and when turned it made an indentation in a paper disk, proving that the patrolman had actually walked the full distance of his patrol.

Cyprus   420 Feet in Length

The steamer Cyprus. *From the collection of William Forsythe and David Huskins.*

As the surfman walked along the shore, he searched the horizon and the beach for signs that a ship was in trouble; possibly a ship flying a distress flag, or possibly debris from a ship washing up on shore.

If the patrolman sighted a ship too close to shore, he would ignite a Coston Signal. The bright red flare would warn the ship of its error. If a shipwreck was found, the flare would indicate to the people on the ship that their predicament had been discovered and that the Life Saving Service was on the way.

The beach patrol walked their assigned route every night, in any weather; spring rain, summer's heat or winter's deep snow until the end of the shipping season.

On a stormy October night of 1907, two patrolmen at the Deer Park Life Saving Station, on the southern shore of Lake Superior in Michigan's Upper Peninsula, pulled on their government issued vests and long pea-coat style coats to ward off the cold fall Lake Superior winds, and oilskins to protect them from the gale blowing in from the northwest. The men started off from the station in opposite directions on their midnight to 4:00 AM beach patrol watch.

They walked along the beach listening to the roar of the large waves crashing on shore. The storm winds blew horizontal sheets of rain obscuring the patrolmen's view of any ship on the lake.

About 2:00 AM the man patrolling east of the station came upon a badly damaged ship's raft, which had been tossed up on the beach. Nearby he found the body of a seaman. The man was alive, but barely.

A Life Saving Surfman on beach patrol. From the Coast Guard Historians Office.

Finding the raft and a lone sailor reminded the men of the Deer Park Station of the wreck of the Western Reserve which they worked fifteen years earlier.

The Western Reserve was the first steel freighter built on the Great lakes and the ship was severely criticized by sailors and builders of traditional wood ships.

On August 30, 1892 the 301-foot long steamer Western Reserve was traveling west on Lake Superior in ballast with a crew of 21, the ship's owner and wife, their two children and two other passengers. The owner was known for having his personal railroad car put on tracks mounted on the ship so he could travel aboard the ship in the luxury he was accustomed to.

The ship encountered a summer storm on Lake Superior. The storm wasn't anything out of the ordinary for the time of year and nothing that would keep other ships from sailing. About 35 miles northwest of the Deer Park Life Saving Station the ship without warning simply broke in two! The steel used in building the ship was not of the correct tensile strength making it brittle. The ship simply did not flex with the movement of the waves.

All aboard the ship took to the ship's yawls to abandon the sinking vessel. Within minutes of being lowered one of the yawls capsized in the storm tossed seas. The nine people thrown from the boat frantically tried to swim through the wind

An example of a Life Saving Service Patrol Clock. From the authors collection.

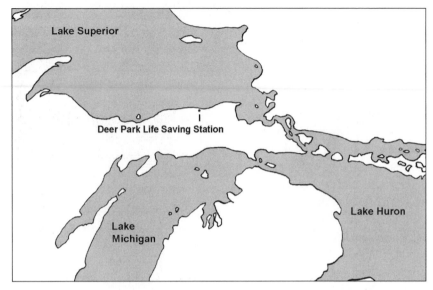

and waves to the other yawl, but only one person was able to make it, and he was pulled aboard.

The small boat with its frightened 19 passengers was at the mercy of the wind and waves. They prayed they would be found and rescued from the storm but they knew that no one knew of their peril, no one was looking for them.

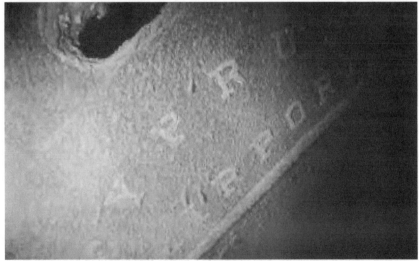

An underwater photograph of the stern of the steamer Cyprus. *Courtesy of the Great Lakes Shipwreck Historical Society.*

The yawl was blown by the relentless wind seas for over ten hours until they were about one mile off shore. As they came closer to shore they could hear the roar of the waves breaking on the huge rocks near shore. A particularly large wave picked up the yawl and threw it down on an offshore sandbar. The small boat came to a sudden stop and the 19 frightened passengers were thrown into the tumultuous lake.

A patrolman from the Deer Park Station happened across the life boat washed up on shore. The nearly dead body of the ship's wheelsman was found close by. He was the only survivor.

Now 15 years later the patrolman was thinking that history was repeating itself as he carried and dragged another nearly dead man back to the Deer Park station. Second Mate Charles Pitz, the sole survivor of the sinking, was unconscious and hypothermic

Charles Pitz, second mate and sole survivor of the steamer Cyprus. *Courtesy of Captain Ann Sanborn.*

from the cold Lake Superior water. He wore a life jacket with a name stenciled on it. The name was *Cyprus*.

The men of the Life Saving Station were confounded, the *Cyprus* couldn't be in trouble. The *Cyprus* was considered one of the best ships on the lakes, she was one of the largest, and she was a new ship. The *Cyprus* was only on her second voyage! The *Cyprus* couldn't have run into trouble in the typical fall storm.

The *Cyprus* was built by the American Shipbuilding Company at their Lorain, Ohio yard. At 420-feet in length and 52-feet wide the steel propeller freighter was one of the largest ships to sail on the Great Lakes at the time.

After intensive nursing, Second Mate Charles Pitz regained consciousness and told of the horror he and the crew faced on Lake Superior.

In the storm, the *Cyprus* was pounded by the northwest waves but she was holding her own in the storm while they made way along the normal east-west course. But, Pitz said, about 7:00 PM while the ship was off Deer Park, the cargo shifted in the heavy seas and the *Cyprus* developed a worsening list as water started leaking into the cargo hold from the hatches.

Captain Huyck didn't panic. He was confident that his new ship could make it to the shelter behind Whitefish Point, where they would ride out the storm, pump out the water, re-distribute the cargo and be on their way.

The captain didn't have concern, the engines were running and the pumps were pumping out thousands of gallons of water per minute. An order to lower lifeboats or for the crew to put on lifejackets was never given.

Suddenly without warning, at 7:00 PM, the ship rolled on her side and almost instantly plunged to the bottom. Anyone below decks was carried to an icy Lake Superior grave. The crew on deck were tossed into the water, most died in minutes from exposure to the cold water.

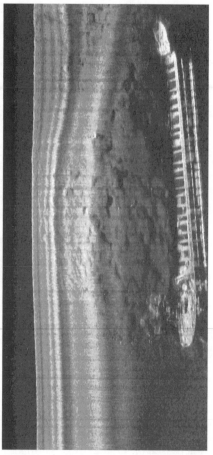

The side scan sonar image of the Cyprus. *She lies on her port side and the hull appears to be fully intact. Courtesy of the Great Lakes Shipwreck Historical Society.*

The raft located forward on the ship floated free as the *Cyprus* capsized. The captain, first mate, wheelsman and Pitz were thrown into the lake. As they came to the surface, they found themselves in towering seas and gale force winds. They frantically swam through the freezing cold water towards the raft. It took all of their remaining strength to climb aboard the raft as it was heaved about by the waves and wind.

The men laid in the raft while it was tossed by the waves, the wind blown rain stung their faces and they feared the raft would overturn and throw them into the lake during the dark stormy night.

Almost seven hours after the *Cyprus* capsized, the raft was blown within a few hundred feet of shore. The waves breaking in the shallows flipped the raft and the men, weakened from their ordeal, were again thrown into the storm tossed sea. The men benumbed by cold, fought to climb back onto the raft, only to be thrown out as the raft overturned again, five times in all. W h e n the men were thrown out, sometimes one would succumb to the cold and not make it back. The pounding surf carried them helplessly in the churning surf and beat them into the rocks along the shore. Only Charles Pitz was able to climb on the raft as the waves threw it up on the beach.

On October 7, 1907 the *Cyprus*, on only her second trip of her career, had taken on 8,000 tons of iron ore at Superior, Wisconsin and departed into a stormy Lake Superior heading to a Buffalo, New York steel mill. The storm was of average velocity, nothing to hold a large steamer in port. But that night the new large *Cyprus* went to the bottom of Lake Superior.

There was much discussion as to what had happened to the *Cyprus*. Mr. Pitz said the ship capsized when the cargo, 8,000 tons of iron ore, had shifted causing the ship to list and take on water. But, many Great Lake sailors charge that the ship was not properly prepared for a storm. The captain did not order the canvas storm tarpaulins to cover the hatch opening before the hatch covers were replaced. In the high seas the waves broke over the deck and leaked into the hold. The water accumulated in the cargo holds.

In support of this theory was Captain Harbottle of the steamer Stephenson that passed the *Cyprus* that fateful night. He said the *Cyprus* left a rusty wake, indicating water had permeated the cargo and carried the ore dust out through the pumps.

Apparently the pumps could not keep up with the volume coming in and the ship rolled under the excess weight

The cause of the sinking of the Great Lakes newest ship is still open to speculation. Yet the result is a known fact; the big new ship had disappeared below Lake Superior taking with her all but one of her crew.

Authors note: During August of 2007 a research team from Great Lakes Shipwreck Historical Society (www.shipwreckmuseum.com/) was searching for the remains of the Great Lakes steamer D.M. Clemson *that sank during a storm in 1908. Through the use of digital side scan sonar equipment they located an unidentified ship on the bottom of Lake Superior and sent an unmanned submersible with video and still cameras to survey the wreck. When the camera photographed the stern of the ship the research team was astonished to find, it wasn't the* Clemson *they had found, it was the* Cyprus.

Almost one hundred years after the ship, on only her second trip, was overcome by a Lake Superior storm. The team from Great Lakes Shipwreck Historical Society had discovered the final resting place of the steamer Cyprus; *460-feet below the surface and about 8 miles north of Deer Park.*

HENRY STEINBRENNER

The 427-foot *Henry Steinbrenner*, owned by the Kingman Transit Company, and operated by her namesake Henry Steinbrenner, was designed and built for carrying iron ore from the rich ore deposits in Minnesota and Michigan to the steel complexes in the lower lakes. The *Steinbrenner* had a long 52-year career on the lakes, but it was a career that was marred by a few "incidents."

The first of the problems for the *Steinbrenner* occurred in 1909 when she collided with the steamer *Harry A. Berwind*. The *Steinbrenner* was holed and sank to the bottom of the St. Marys River. Since winter was approaching the ship was left where she sank, on the bottom. She was later raised, repaired and went back to work on the lakes.

Twelve years later, in 1923, the *Steinbrenner* was again involved in a collision. This time it was in Lake Superior's Whitefish Bay with the vessel *John McCartney*. The *Steinbrenner* was damaged but made it safely to a shore facility. She was again taken out of service for repairs.

Henry Steinbrenner   427 Feet in Length

The Steinbrenner *being raised after her 1909 sinking. From the Edwin Brown collection of the State of Michigan Archives, Lansing, Michigan.*

The next "incident" transpired in 1941. The *Steinbrenner* was again in the St. Marys River entering the Soo Locks when she rammed the lock wall and was so damaged that the ship had to be once again taken out of service.

The *Henry Steinbrenner* remained on the lakes until 1953, without any further significant "incidents."

On May 10, 1953 at 5:01 AM the *Steinbrenner* departed Superior, Wisconsin with a cargo of iron ore. The iron ore was headed to feed the insatiable demands of the steel industry on Lake Erie.

When the ship departed, the weather was calm with no sea running. The forecast was for a south southwest wind to develop and reach a velocity of 30-35 miles per hour. There was also a possibility for thunder squalls in the western portion of the lake. The weather was nothing that would hold the *Steinbrenner* in port.

The ship's cargo holds were equipped with hatch covers, each held down with twenty eight clamps. During heavy water, a canvas tarpaulin was fitted over the cargo opening before the hatch covers were clamped on. This step helped to keep the lake water from seeping in through the hatches.

The weather forecasts weren't calling for conditions so drastic that would require tarps, so they were left off.

About 3:00 PM, ten hours into the trip, the wind began to freshen and the waves increased. Captain Albert Stiglin, master of the *Steinbrenner*, radioed that the seas were building and they were taking green water over the bow.

The weather forecast was still predicting south southwest winds but the forecasters had increased the velocity slightly to 30-40 miles per hour. Still nothing that would chase most Great Lakes freighters into shelter.

Crew was sent out to tighten the cargo hatch cover clamps. The order was also given to check and secure all deadlights and hawse pipe covers. These orders were typical precautionary measures taken when the weather kicked up.

Around 8:00 on the evening of May 10 the storm worked one of the cargo hatch covers loose.

The third mate and three deckhands volunteered to go on deck and tighten the clamps. The ship was rolling in the seas and the waves breaking on the deck sent a spray up that could easily knock a man off his feet.

Since the conditions were so bad on deck the men wore a harness with a travel line connected to the ship's deck lifeline. The men braced themselves and walked in a wide stance trying to keep from being blown from the deck. Between the wind and the waves washing the deck, the task the men were to accomplish would be tedious at best.

The Henry Steinbrenner. *From the Edwin Brown collection of the State of Michigan Archives, Lansing, Michigan.*

At one point during the repair a particularly large wave broke over the ship and sent torrents of water rushing aft. The men were tightening the clamps when the wave struck. They could not help themselves from being washed away by the volume of water that poured aft along the deck. The men tumbled along the deck, thankful they were secured to the ship by the lifeline or they would have been washed over. If any of the men were washed off the deck into the sea, the conditions were so bad that the *Steinbrenner* could not have come about to rescue them.

As the men recovered from the wash that took them off their feet, they realized one of the men was missing. They worked their way back to the cargo hold and found the missing man, Tom Wells, hanging from his travel line in the cargo hold.

The horrible wind and huge waves tossing the ship as if it were a child's toy, the men struggled to pull on Tom's travel line, hauling him out of the hold and back on deck.

The men staggered on the rolling deck of the ship, aft to the galley / dining room. There they took time to regain their strength and were warmed by the cook's hot coffee. Once recuperated, the men went back out into the elements to fasten down the hatch cover clamps. All went back out except Tom Wells. He decided to remain in the galley, safe, warm and dry.

Conditions as bad as they were, they were about to get worse. Throughout the night the wind velocity increased, blowing as high as 80 miles per hour! The seas also continued to grow in height and intensity.

Early in the morning of May 11, the waves crashing down on the ship smashed in a door on the forecastle deck. Shortly thereafter the hatch cover secured by the crew had again worked loose.

With the winds blowing at up to 80 miles per hour and the waves running at 20- to 30-feet the conditions on deck had deteriorated to the extent that men could not be sent out to tighten the loose clamps.

The intense wind ripped at the hawse pipe covers and the clamps, loosening more hatch covers. Water poured in through all openings accumulating in the cargo hold faster than the pumps could remove it.

Captain Stiglin knew his ship was in trouble and decided to maneuver the *Steinbrenner* into a protected position between Isle Royale and Passage Island.

A little past 7:00 AM on May 11, 1953 the captain gave orders to the crew to dress for the cold and put on their life jackets. He then put out a call to any vessels in the vicinity for assistance.

Just a half of an hour later the conditions aboard the *Henry Steinbrenner* worsened. The clamps on the three aft hatches loosened and the covers

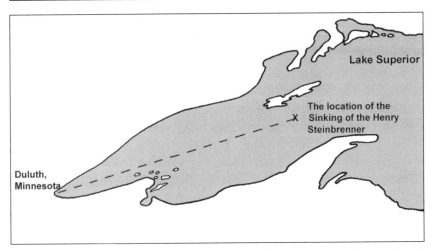

Lake Superior

The location of the
X Sinking of the Henry
Steinbrenner

Duluth,
Minnesota

became dislodged. The mountainous waves broke on the bow of the ship and huge amounts of lake water ran the length of the ship and poured into the now open cargo holds at the aft of the ship.

"Stop the engines!" Captain Stiglin ordered. Then he sent out another message.

The message contained a request for any vessel in the area to come to their help and gave their location as 15 miles due south of the Isle Royale light.

The captain looked aft, and even through the wind blown spray and waves breaking on the ship, he could see his ship was going down by the stern.

The engines were stopped in preparation for the captain's next order... abandon ship!

The last sound a sailor wants to hear is the blaring of the abandon ship alarm.

As the harsh signal blared, the crew, without panic, prepared to abandon ship as they had so often practiced.

The ten crewmembers working at the forward end of the ship assembled on the forecastle deck at the life raft. At the stern the men gathered at the number one and number two lifeboats.

When the abandon ship alarm was sounded the captain also sent out a "Mayday" call to ships in the area and to the Coast Guard to come to their aid.

The ship was rapidly settling stern first as the waves broke over her and poured into the three open aft cargo holds.

The men at the stern readied the two twenty man lifeboats; lifeboat #1 was on the starboard, and on the port side lifeboat #2 hung from its davits.

The starboard lifeboat was swung out in a launch position away from the ship. But it prematurely lowered. The men held the painter, the bowline, but the waves carried the lifeboat away with only seven men aboard.

At the portside lifeboat, Third Assistant Engineer, Arthur Morse, helped other crewmen into the lifeboat. At launch Art refused to get into the boat, rather he elected to remain on the quickly sinking *Steinbrenner*. He knew the lifeboat would require help clearing the hull of the ship, he also knew it couldn't be done from the lifeboat.

As the lifeboat began to lower a holding line that reduces the lifeboat swing had not been disconnected in the rush to get off the sinking ship.

With the holding line attached the lifeboat could not be fully lowered and if the lifeboat remained attached to the ship, the *Steinbrenner* would pull the lifeboat and its passengers to the bottom with her. A quick thinking Art Morse pulled out his pocketknife and cut the line. Art looked at the men and said, "So long boys, and good luck."

That was the last anyone saw of Art.

At the bow Captain Stiglin and nine men struggled to ready the six by twelve foot metal air tank and wood raft. The ship was pitching and rolling and waves broke over the deck hampering their efforts. A large wave crashed down at the bow of the *Steinbrenner*, the torrent of water lifted the raft and smashed it against the pilothouse wall, pinning Joe Radzewicz against the wall. Joe sustained a compound fracture to his left leg and broke his left arm.

Joe Radzewicz was no stranger to having a ship sink from beneath him. He had been aboard the *George M. Humphrey* in 1943 when, after a collision, the *Humphrey* sank in the Straights of Mackinaw.

The D. G. Kerr. *From the H. C. Inches Collection of the Port Huron Museum.*

The Wilfred Sykes. *From the H. C. Inches Collection of the Port Huron Museum.*

As the ship sank lower, the ten men climbed in to the raft and waited for it to float free of the ship. Just as the raft began to float a wave mounted the ship and capsized the raft, the crew were cast into the turbulent sea.

The men frantically swam towards the raft being tossed about on the waves. They struggled to climb back into the raft. The men were freezing and exhausted but they knew their only salvation was the raft. Swimming in cold Lake Superior water during a spring storm 15 miles from the closest land was a sure recipe for death.

Captain Stiglin and five of the men were able to climb back into the safety of the raft.

"… we lost four men for only six climbed back on the raft, including the injured Radzewicz." said Captain Stiglin.

The men could see the lifejackets of the four men but they were empty. Apparently the wicked sea stripped the men of their jackets.

The *Henry Steinbrenner* then slipped beneath the waves.

The men in the lifeboats and raft were off the sinking *Steinbrenner* but their safety was not guaranteed. They were drifting in a raging sea, with hurricane force winds, in sub freezing temperatures. To make matters worse, they didn't know if any ships had received their Mayday call or if they did, how close the ships were to their position or how long it would take for them to arrive on site. They wondered if the lake would take them before help arrived.

Captain Stiglin's request for assistance and the Mayday were heard around the lake. Ships close to the coordinates the captain gave diverted their course and steamed to help. Lake men are quick to assist their brothers of the lakes.

The J. H. Thompson. *From the Hugh Clark Great Lakes Photographic Collection.*

The *D.M. Clemson*, *D. G. Kerr*, *Wilfred Sykes* and *Joseph H. Thomson* were all ships that responded to Captain Stiglin's call for help. The closest to the position of the sinking *Steinbrenner* was 13 miles.

The Captain's frantic radio calls were also received by the Coast Guard and several vessels were sent following the *Steinbrenner's* Mayday.

Coast Guard rescue boats from Grand Marais, Two Harbors, Minnesota, Ashland, Wisconsin, Portage Canal, and Hancock, Michigan were dispatched. An air/and sea rescue airplane from Traverse City, Michigan was also sent to aid in the search.

The men aboard the open boats, drenched by the 35-degree water, suffered terribly. The lifeboats and raft were tossed about by the 20-foot waves as if they were corks. The small boats rose on the crest of the waves but were then thrown into the trough and the men could see nothing but an angry Lake Superior in any direction. The wind, gusting up to 80 miles per hour, blew spray at such velocity it stung the faces of the terrified men.

Sitting low in the lifeboats and raft the men hoped they wouldn't be blown over. They clenched the thwarts and gunnels with ever numbing fingers, with thoughts of wives and children at home, and prayed.

About two hours into their ordeal the Coast Guard airplane was heard by the men. It raised their spirits but they knew the plane couldn't make a water landing in the tremendous seas. But they knew the plane would radio their position to other rescue vessels.

The men had floated helplessly on a wild Lake Superior for over four hours before Great Lake freighters arrived on the scene.

The Joseph Thompson, the largest ship on the lakes in 1953, steamed into sight of the life raft. A rescue by such a large ship in such turbulent seas was going to tax the skills of the Thompson's captain and helmsman.

The huge ship made a head-on approach towards the raft. A crewman aboard the ship threw a heaving line to the raft but the wind and seas caused it to miss its mark.

With great effort the big ship came about and made another approach. This time the heaving line was caught by deckhand James Lambaris aboard the raft.

"I held on for dear life," Lambaris said.

The bobbing raft was worked closer to the ship heaving in the heavy seas. The Jacobs ladder was lowered over the side of the ship to the raft, but the men were too numb and exhausted by exposure to the climactic conditions and shock to climb up to the deck of the ship.

The third mate of the Thompson, without thought of his own safety, descended the ladder swinging wildly and beating against the steel hull of the big ship. He tied lines around four of the survivors and they were hoisted aboard the Thompson. Two other men on the raft needed to be raised to the Thompson's deck by use of a metal stretcher basket.

The Coast Guard boats and the other steamers patrolled the area searching for survivors. The steamer *Clemson* picked up the men, both alive and dead from one of the lifeboats. The ship took on seven survivors and four dead. The *Kerr* found and took on two bodies.

The *Sykes* came across the other lifeboat. The steamer maneuvered until it had the lifeboat along side. A line was attached from the lifeboat to the *Sykes*.

The United States Coast Guard Cutter Woodrush. *From the Richard Wicklund Collection.*

A large wave caught the lifeboat and the line snapped. The steamer had to come about and work its way along the lifeboat again. The two survivors and one dead sailor were quickly removed from the lifeboat before the waves drove it away again.

The Coast Guard cutter *Woodrush* remained onsite overnight while the smaller Coast Guard boats went to shore. The steamers concluded their search and continued on to their destinations; the *Sykes* to Superior, Wisconsin, the Thompson, *Clemson* and *Kerr* to the locks at Sault Ste. Marie, Michigan.

The sinking of the *Henry Steinbrenner* in the early spring of 1953 brought the end to the 52 year old ship. Fourteen of her crew survived the trying ordeal, 10 bodies were recovered and seven men were reported missing and presumed dead.

There was praise heaped on Art Morse for his heroism and self sacrifice.

The men said that Captain Stiglin had done all he could in trying to save the ship and crew. Yet, under interrogation at the official Coast Guard Inquiry, two of the crew said that many of the clamps securing the hatch cover had stripped threads which did not allow the clamps to be adequately tightened. A watchman went as far to claim that the *Steinbrenner* should not have been sailing.

"Nothing worked aboard the ship as it should have. We were taking water something awful for nearly 13 hours before she went down. For my money, she just wasn't seaworthy."

A United States Coast Guard Board of Inquiry was assembled to determine the cause of the foundering of the *Henry Steinbrenner*.

After an extensive investigation the Board released its findings. They found that the heavy seas had dislodged the three cargo hatches, numbers 10, 11, and 12. The dislodging of the covers permitted water to enter the ship and flood the cargo holds.

The accusation that the clamps were stripped and not capable of adequately securing the hatch covers was discussed at length. The Board found through testimony that there were only a few stripped clamps and they were wrapped with marlin that allowed them to be clamped tightly. The Board also found that the sea conditions could work the clamps loose, but the Board did indicate that the use of tarpaulins would have helped clamp the hatch covers tighter

The ultimate conclusion was that the foundering of the *Henry Steinbrenner* causing the death of ten of her crew was the result of an act of God.

SHIPS AT LEAST 400 FEET
THE SHIPS OF NOVEMBER 1913

As sure as there is snow in the winter, fall storms will occur on the Great Lakes. November is well known for its horrendous storms that turn the Great Lakes into a boiling cauldron of wind and waves.

Every fall there are storms of intense velocity but there is one storm that stands far out from the others, the "Great Storm of 1913."

The 1913 storm, referred to as a "White Hurricane"; a storm on freshwater with winds of hurricane intensity, is widely recognized as the worst storm to ever take aim on the Great Lakes, in terms of the number of dead and missing sailors and the destruction of ships.

The storm began as a weak low-pressure Arctic front coming down in a southeast direction from Canada. On November 8, 1913 the government Weather Bureau issued a storm warning for the Great Lakes and the square red flags with a black center square were raised at all ports along the lakes to tell mariners of the impending storm.

The warnings did not hold most ships in port. It was towards the end of the season and the captains were under pressure from the shipping companies to make as many trips as possible before winter ice closed the season.

In addition to the Arctic front bearing down on the lakes there was an intense storm system tracking north from the Appalachian Mountains. As it neared the Arctic front the warmer southern storm changed course towards the northwest as it began to absorb the cold air. The southern storm, heavy with moisture, combined with the cold Arctic air over the Great Lakes basin.

Lakes Michigan and Superior fell victim to the intense winds, gigantic waves and snow squalls of the Arctic front. Lake Erie was assaulted by the leading edge of the southern storm but Lake Huron was pounded by the full brunt of the combined storms.

Lakeside communities in Michigan and Ontario were paralyzed with up to 2-feet of snow and the high winds caused drifts several feet high.

Storms of this magnitude usually last for four or five hours then pass on, but the storm of November 1913 wreaked havoc on the lakes for over three days!

Most smaller ships sought shelter during the storm but several large Great Lakes steamships ventured out on lakes even though storm warnings had been issued.

The captains of the large steel ships relied on their knowledge of the lakes, weather and the waves. They also had great confidence in their vessels. But, they had never sailed into a storm of such catastrophic proportions as the storm that assaulted the lakes on those November days.

Ships that had successfully sailed through the storm later related the horror they endured during the passage. The waves crashed down on the length of the ship, the winds that threatened to blow the ship into the trough of the waves, windows in pilothouses and skylights of engine rooms smashed, lifeboats ripped from their davits and the violent rolling and pitching of the ships in the 30 plus foot seas.

The storm wreaked havoc on the lakes for three days leaving in its wake 19 vessels either cast aground or lost and at least 235 sailors killed. The exact number will never be known.

The following are the ships of at least 400-feet in length that were out on the lake and assaulted by the storm.

Argus   436 Feet in Length

The 436-foot steel freighter *Argus* was only 10 tears old at the time of her loss. As she steamed on Lake Huron along the Canadian shore the *Argus* broke in half and sank near Kincardin, Ontario taking her crew of twenty five with her.

The *Hydrus*, like the *Argus*, was 436-feet in length and also launched in 1903. The *Hydrus* was down-bound along the Michigan shore with a cargo of

Hydrus   436 Feet in Length

The Hydrus. *From the Collection of Marine Artist Robert McGreevy,*
http://www.mcgreevy.com.

iron ore in winds nearing 90 miles per hour and waves taller than a three-
story building.

The huge steel ship weighed down by its cargo probably became trapped
in the trough of the waves, its cargo shifted and she rolled over and sank off
Lexington, Michigan with her crew of twenty eight.

John A. McGean

The five year old, *John A. McGean,* was a steel 452-foot steamer when she
slipped beneath the surface of Lake Huron. During the White Hurricane the

John A. McGean   452 Feet in Length

The John A. McGean. *From the collections of the Port Huron Museum.*

big ship was last seen heading north not far from Saginaw Bay. The ship disappeared with its cargo of coal and crew of twenty eight.

On Lake Superior the 472-foot long steamer *L.C. Waldo* had taken on a cargo of iron ore on the western end of Lake Superior. As the *Waldo* made its way through the storm the ship was buffeted by high wind and waves. The captain of the *Waldo* was anxious to get behind the Keweenaw Peninsula to anchor in its shelter.

Blinded by the blizzard conditions the *Waldo* misjudged its position and ran aground on Gull Island located between Passage Island and Keweenaw Point.

 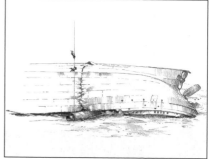

The McGean *as it appears on the bottom of Lake Huron. From the collection of Great Lakes Marine artist Robert McGreevy, http://www.mcgreevy.com.*

L. C. Waldo   472 Feet in Length

The giant waves beat down on the stern of the grounded ship destroying its after deck house. The crew gathered in the bow awaiting rescue. The Eagle Bay and Portage Life Saving Stations both made several attempts to get to the stricken vessel but were chased back by the storm.

The crew, hungry and cold, remained on the *Waldo* for four days while the waves crashed down on the ship before they were rescued.

The badly damaged ship was declared a total loss but was eventually removed, repaired and put back into service. Her career lasted another 54 years, sailing as the *Waldo*, *Riverton* and the *Mohawk Deer*.

During the Storm of 1913 the *Howard M. Hanna Jr.*, a 480-foot steel bulk freighter, was carrying a load of coal north on Lake Huron. The five year old

The Mohawk Deer *passing through Port Huron. From the Great Lakes Collection of Hugh Clark.*

Howard H. Hanna   480 Feet in Length

ship passed the Huron Lightship as it entered the southern end of Lake Huron and passed into the history books as a ship that survived the Great Storm.

The *Hanna* worked its way north into the increasingly violent northeast storm, giant waves swept over the ship. Crewmen huddling in the after cabins listened to the terrible sounds of lines snapping, the screeching of metal being twisted and broken as the starboard lifeboats were ripped from their davits and the roof of the aft cabin being blown off.

In the pilothouse, the helmsman and officers were not spared the storm's savage fury. As the bow of the ship crashed into the monstrous waves the pilothouse was pounded by the energy stored in the wall of water.

The helmsman held onto the wheel for support as the ship at an almost 60 degree incline climbed the waves, when suddenly a wall of water crashed down on the ship, smashing the pilothouse windows and filling the pilothouse with cold Lake Huron water. The winds gusting to 90 miles per hour then tore off the roof of the pilothouse.

The Howard M. Hanna *on the Port Austin reef after being ravaged by the Great Storm of 1913. Library of Congress, Prints and Photographs Division, Detroit Publishing Company Collection.*

The Port Austin Reef Lighthouse. From the authors collection.

The *Hanna* was crossing Saginaw Bay when Captain Hagen wished he had sought the shelter at the government Harbor of Refuge at Harbor Beach, but there was no way he could turn back in the conditions.

When a tremendous wave crashed down on the *Hanna*. Captain Hagen found it impossible to keep the *Hanna* heading into the waves. Each wave crashing into the vessel pushed the bow to port. Until the storm won the battle and the *Hanna* swung into the trough and became trapped broadside in the waves and was subjected to a terrible pounding along its length. The ship rolled violently from port to starboard with the onslaught of each wave.

The wind and waves were so great the *Hanna* was pushed up on the rocky Port Austin reef less than 1000-feet east of the Port Austin Reef Light.

The stranded ship now received the full brunt of the waves. Mountains of water smashed down onto the hapless ship tearing off all of her hatch covers and allowing thousands of gallons of lake water to pour into her hold.

Above the roar of the storm, the popping of rivets and the metal deck plates being ripped could be heard. The ship had broken in two!

The following day the seas and the storm had subsided to the extent that some of the crew could take to the lifeboats and make it to shore. But, the *Hanna*, it was declared a total constructive loss.

In the weeks and months that followed, salvager Tom Reid was able to re-float and rebuilt the *Hanna* putting her back into service. The *Howard M. Hanna Jr.* sailed the Great Lakes for another 70 years!

The sinking of the 524-foot *Charles S. Price* was shocking to most mariners. How could such a large ship, just three years old, be sunk by a mere storm?

The *Price* was north-bound with a cargo of coal, storm warning flags flew and the storm was lashing the lake but the big newer ship entered Lake Huron anyway. The captain and crew had confidence in their ship.

The Charles S. Price. *From the collections of the Port Huron Museum.*

The *Price* plowed into the wind and waves for almost 60 miles, nearing Saginaw Bay when apparently the *Price* tried to come about and return to the safety of the St. Clair River.

A large ship was later found floating bottom up in Lake Huron near Port Huron, Michigan. When the weather calmed, the Reid Wrecking and Towing Company tug *Sarnia City* went to the capsized hull. Lewis Meyers donned his hard hat diving suit and under the supervision of Tom Reid was lowered down to determine the name of the mystery vessel. He came up with the news: *Charles S. Price.*

The capsized hulk of a Great Lakes steamer was found floating in lower Lake Huron. From the State of Michigan Archives, Lansing Michigan.

Charles S. Price   524 Feet in Length

Isaac M. Scott   524 Feet in Length

The *Price*, only three years old, had "turned turtle" in the violent storm of November 1913, a testament to the strength and fury of the storm. Her crew of 28 had perished in the disaster. In the following days their bodies began washing up on the Canadian shore.

Also out in the storm was the sister ship of the *Price*, the Isaac M. Scott. The Scott, 524-feet in length and only four years old was steaming up Lake Huron with a load of coal. The ship fought for hours through the brunt of the

A post card showing the Henry B. Smith *in Ashtabula, Ohio. From the collection of William Forsythe and David Huskins.*

Henry B. Smith   545 Feet in Length

storm until the "White Hurricane" finally got the best of the big ship. It's not known what happened, for there were not any witnesses left alive to tell, but the Isaac M. Scott went down with all twenty eight crew about seven miles northeast of Thunder Bay.

The 545-foot, seven year old, *Henry B. Smith* had taken on a cargo of iron ore at Marquette, Michigan and on November 9th ventured out into stormy Lake Superior.

The captain of a ship docked at Marquette watched the *Henry B. Smith* apparently attempting to turn around and return to the shelter of Marquette harbor. The *Smith* rolled violently in the seas and wind until she could no longer be seen through the blizzard.

The *Henry B. Smith* never arrived at the Soo Locks. The ship never cleared Lake Superior. The *Smith* and her crew of twenty five went down in Lake Superior north of Marquette.

The 550-foot *James C. Carruthers* was the largest ship to be lost in the Great Storm of 1913. The ship was also the newest, for the ship was in her first season on the lakes.

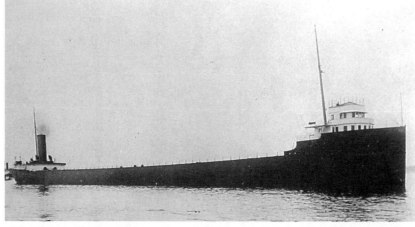

The James C. Carruthers. *From the collections of the Port Huron Museum.*

James C. Carruthers 550 Feet in Length

The huge ship was carrying over 10,000 tons of wheat when it is theorized that she was blown into the trough of the sea, was unable to recover and eventually succumbed to the horrendous storm. The big *Carruthers* was later found off Kincardine, Ontario. The ship took her twenty five man crew to their deaths.

It's hard to conceive that a mere storm could cause large ships to sink to the bottom, but the storm of 1913 is testament to the power of nature.

SHIPS AT LEAST 400 FEET
E.M. FORD

In 1979 the *E.M. Ford* had reached the ripe old age of 81 years. For a Great Lakes freighter battling 81 seasons of storm tossed waves, early spring ice and millions of tons of cargo poured into and taken out of her hold, that is pretty darn good.

The ship was built in 1898 for the Cleveland Cliffs Company as the steamer Presque Isle. She sailed with the company until 1955 when she was sold. After modifications, the 428-foot ship was re-christened the *E.M. Ford*.

On the evening of December 25, 1979 a storm bore down on Lake Michigan with 15 to 20-foot seas. While not pleasant for the crew, the *E.M. Ford* could handle it. Over her career she had seen worse storms. Unfortunately for the ship, she was not out on the open lake where she could ride out the storm. She was moored at the Jones Island dock at Milwaukee, Wisconsin.

On that Christmas day on 1979, the *E.M. Ford* was tied up to a dock. The ship had arrived two days prior with 7,000 tons of cargo from Alpena, Michigan. Because of the holiday, the cargo was not scheduled to be

E. M. Ford   453 Feet in Length

The E.M. Ford. *From the Great Lakes Photographic Collection of Hugh Clark.*

unloaded until later in the week and most of the crew of 30 departed to spend Christmas with their families. Only five men stayed behind to keep watch aboard the docked ship.

The winds blew ferociously up to 60 miles per hour. The *Ford* was rolled at the dock under the force of the wind until one at a time the 16 mooring lines, made up from 4-1/2 inch nylon rope and 1 inch steel cable, snapped under the stress. The big ship then was shoved around by the wind.

The *E.M. Ford* smashed into the dock repeatedly, crashing against the sturdy steel covered concrete structure. The five men onboard made a frantic call for help. They were afraid the ship would be beaten into pieces, taking them along with it. A tugboat came to their assistance, maneuvered close and removed the crew, but the wind and waves continued to smash the ship against the dock.

Attempts were made to secure the *Ford*. Cables were made fast to the ship and winches were used to pull it away from the dock wall. More cables were added to stabilize the vessel but the damage had been done.

While the ship was repeatedly pounded against the dock, a 24-foot gash was torn in the ship's starboard bow. Along the port side cracks appeared in the hull, some up to 12-feet long.

The ship began taking on water. Slowly the *E.M. Ford* settled. When the storm subsided, the freighter was found lying on the bottom.

An initial examination revealed that water had entered the engine room. The gashes in the hull would need to be temporarily repaired and much of the water pumped out before the *Ford* could be moved to a dry dock for permanent repairs.

The E.M. Ford *sits on the bottom at the Jones Island Dock. Photograph by Norbert Huskins, E.M. Ford Chief Engineer. Provided by David Huskins.*

Once the ship had been raised it was discovered that water had gotten into the cargo hold and that the ship's cargo had become wet. The *E.M. Ford's* cargo of 7,000 tons of dry cement had crusted over. A three foot thick crust of cement had formed in the cargo hold!

Before the ship could be repaired several tons of hardened cement had to be broken out with jackhammers. The process took weeks.

Ironically, the ship that sunk and became the butt of many jokes; "The Concrete Freighter", "The Cement Mixer", "The ship that floats like a rock", is still afloat.

The *E.M. Ford* holds the distinction of being the oldest ship still operating on the Great Lakes. The *E.M. Ford* is at this writing tied up in the Saginaw River for use as a floating cement storage container at 109 years old.

SHIPS AT LEAST 400 FEET
M/V MONTROSE

The Detroit River connects Lake Erie at its south end up approximately 28 miles to Lake St. Clair at the north and is bordered by Canada's Ontario Province on the east and Michigan in the United States on the west side.

The river is a major waterway connecting the Great Lakes. Any ship traveling between Lakes Michigan, Huron or Superior and Lakes Ontario and Erie must pass through the Detroit River.

When the St. Lawrence Seaway was opened to the Great Lakes, both foreign and Great Lakes ships could transport cargo into and out of the lakes to ports around the world.

The increase of foreign ships on the lakes caused some problems due to the foreign sailors not being familiar with the lakes and not being familiar with the rules governing Great Lakes commercial ship traffic.

The Canadian and United States governments made laws that any ship of foreign registry must have aboard a Canadian or United States licensed Great Lakes Pilot when operating in the Great Lakes.

M/V Montrose   444 Feet in Length

The Ambassador Bridge crossing the Detroit River between Detroit, Michigan and Windsor, Ontario. From the Hugh Clark Photograph collection of the Great Lakes.

The 444-foot British freighter, *Montrose*, was on her fifth trip into the lakes in July of 1962. On this trip the one-year-old vessel, whose homeport is London, was docked at the Detroit Harbor Terminal taking on a cargo of 200 tons of aluminum.

At 9:00 PM on July 30, 1962 the *Montrose* had completed taking on cargo and was preparing to depart bound to Fort William, Ontario on Lake Superior. On the bridge of the *Montrose* were the ship's master, Captain Ralph Eyre-Walker and George Beatty, a Canadian Great Lakes Pilot.

They were in communication with the up-bound T. J. McCarthy, an automobile carrier which was waiting for the *Montrose* to depart so she could hug the western side of the river and make a wide swing towards the east to her dock.

At 9:20 PM on a warm, clear evening the *Montrose* cast off lines and left the dock heading across the down-bound shipping lane to the northbound lane.

Captain Eyre-Walker felt his ship was not clearing the dock fast enough for the incoming T.J. McCarthy and called for full speed as they headed across the river.

The quiet of the evening was suddenly filled with a series of blasts from a ship whistle.

The 65-foot tugboat *B.H. Becker* was on the river making one of its five trips per week from the Peerless Cement plant in Port Huron to the Peerless plant located on the Detroit River in River Rouge, Michigan.

The tug carried a crew of four; Captain Fuller, wheelsman McLean, and two deck hands, Hugh McDonald and Gordon Watson. All four were on duty preparing for docking.

On the evening of July 30, 1962 the *Becker* was traveling in the down-bound lane pushing the 200-foot barge, ABL 502, filled with 1,600 tons of clinker cement (a by-product of making Portland Cement) towards the Ambassador Bridge.

Captain Fuller, at the wheel, looked out over the river and the lights of Downtown Detroit and the Ambassador Bridge reflecting off the river. There was a variety of foreign ships on the river, five were tied at the Detroit Harbor Terminal and four others were at anchor awaiting dock space.

While enjoying the warm July evening, Captain Fuller was shocked as a large ship off his starboard bow pulled away from the dock on the American side and began to cross the down-bound shipping lane.

Captain Fuller reached up and sounded several sharp warning blasts on the tug's whistle and with his other hand reached for the radio to call the large ship crossing his bow to warn them of their presence.

Several more warning blasts were sounded from the tug, then Captain Fuller threw the engines into reverse to slow the tug's forward movement. Wheelsman McLean shined the tug's powerful spotlight on the barge, lighting it as if it were daylight, trying to alert the ship of the tug and barge.

The T. J. McCarthy *during winter lay-up. Her automobile deck can be seen above the spar deck. From the Great Lakes Photograph collection of Hugh Clark.*

The British freighter Montrose *grounded beneath the Ambassador Bridge after colliding with a barge being pushed by a tug. Photograph from the collections of the State of Michigan Archives.*

Captain Eyre-Walker and the Great Lakes Pilot Beatty had looked upriver and seeing no traffic, cast off their lines and proceeded across the down-bound lane towards the up-bound lane.

It wasn't until they heard the whistle blasts and the spotlight lit the barge that a lookout screamed, "Barge!" and the men on the *Montrose's* bridge became aware of the down-bound tug and barge.

The corner of the barge's heavily reinforced square bow struck the *Montrose* tearing a hole 48-foot long and up to 24-foot wide in the foreign ship's forward hull.

Captain Fuller immediately radioed the Coast Guard informing them of the collision.

The crew on the tug quickly put on their life preservers and ran to the bow of the barge to check the damage. They were ready to use axes to chop the lines connecting the tug to the barge if the barge was in danger of sinking. They didn't want the barge filled with 1,600 tons of cement to sink and pull the tug down with it. The port bow was quite mangled but fortunately the barge was not taking on water.

The hull of the Montrose *resting on the bottom of the Detroit River. From the Hugh Clark Photograph collection of the Great Lakes.*

Almost immediately after the collision, the *Montrose* began to heel over to port from the volume of water pouring in through the gash. Captain Eyre-Walker knew his ship was sinking and directed the ship to be beached in the shallow water on the Canadian side.

The water rushing in near the bow caused the bow to lower and the stern to rise to the point its propellers were out of the water. With no propulsion the current of the river caught the sinking *Montrose* and carried it downstream

The Montrose *lying on the bottom of the Detroit River. From the collections of the Port Huron Museum.*

The Montrose *near the river bank during the salvage process. From the collections of the Port Huron Museum.*

until it grounded beneath the Ambassador Bridge and rolled over on her side settling in 35-feet of water.

The accident occurred within sight of the docks for Detroit fireboat, *John Kendal* and the mail boat, *J. W. Westcott*. Both vessels hurriedly left their dock to lend assistance. The *John Kendal* circled the *Montrose* looking for any signs of fire while the *Westcott*, the Detroit Harbor Master's launch and a Coast Guard boat took the crew off the ship.

In the collision of the *Montrose* and the barge pushed by the *B.H. Becker* there were no fatalities and the injuries were minor. But the hull of the one year old foreign freighter blocked part of the shipping lanes in one of the busiest waterways on the Great Lakes.

The Canadian Great Lakes pilot aboard the *Montrose* claimed that he had made the required security radio call alerting all boat traffic in their vicinity that they were about to leave the dock and cross the down-bound lane. He also said the barge did not show the required red and green lights and that the tug did not sound an emergency whistle blast.

Several witnesses to the collision refuted these claims. The men on the *John Kendal* and *Westcott* said they heard the whistle and saw the red and green lights on the barge.

Captain A. J. Chickonoski of the automobile carrier *T.J. McCarthy*, the closest ship to the accident, testified that no radio call was heard and he

The raising of the sunken Montrose. *From the collections of the Port Huron Museum.*

could clearly see the lights of the tug and barge from his position behind the *Montrose*.

While the Coast Guard began its investigation into the cause of the accident, a very expensive salvage operation was undertaken. Over a two month period, the 200 tons of aluminum cargo was removed, cables were attached to the ship and it was pulled sideways to the river bank. Once near the bank, the ship was fitted with a temporary patch, pumps dewatered the hull and a crane lifted the ship to an upright position.

The one year old British ship on her fifth trip to the Great Lakes was involved in a collision while crossing the down-bound shipping lane of the Detroit River. The *Montrose* was towed to Lorain, Ohio where she was repaired. And the *Montrose* never returned to the Great Lakes.

SHIPS AT LEAST 400 FEET
CITY OF BANGOR

Captain Edward Recor, master of the 286-foot *Thomas Maytham*, stood at the bridge of his ship peering out the windows, although, he couldn't see much beyond the bow of his ship with the blizzard blowing. The ship carried a cargo of 120,000 bushels of wheat from Duluth, Minnesota destined for Toledo, Ohio; a trip which would cover almost 600 miles.

About 200 miles into the trip on the wintry day of December 1, 1926, a storm was blowing across Lake Superior from the southwest. The storm with 45-50 mile per hour winds blew the lake into a frenzy; waves grew large and beat down on any ship that had not yet sought the shelter of a harbor, cove or in the lee of a land mass.

Ships caught out on the water, like the *Maytham* fought to keep their bow into the waves and battled to hold their course in the zero visibility blizzard.

As the waves crashed over the bow, the entire length of the ship was awash with freezing cold Lake Superior water, Captain Recor decided to seek shelter behind the lee of the Keweenaw Peninsula. The course change was made and the ship slowly came to port. The master of the *Maytham* found conditions

City of Bangor   445 Feet in Length

not much better but he knew the further the ship traveled the more protection the peninsula would offer.

On Wednesday morning nothing was visible out the pilothouse windows but white. The wheelsman strained against the power of the wind and seas to maintain the ship on course. The bow high attitude of the ship followed by the stern high plunge continued, until the ship rose as she had all night and on the downward plunge struck the bottom!

The crew flew from their braced positions with the sudden grinding stop of the ship. The big steel ship had climbed a wave and was thrown down hard on a reef.

The *Maytham* hard aground was now pounded by the waves. Without the cushion of water to absorb the energy of the waves, the ship received the full brunt of the huge seas crashing down on her, threatening to break the ship up with each wave that beat down on her. A coating of ice began to form on the ship adding to the weight of the vessel.

Captain Recor ordered the ship to be lightened. By discharging some of the cargo the ship might become buoyant enough that the *Maytham* could power off the reef.

Crewmen toiling in subfreezing temperatures in the howling wind, and spray that drenched their clothes and froze to their faces jettisoned five hundred bushels of wheat over the side using only hand shovels.

But the waves had pushed the ship hard on the reef and even with less weight in cargo the ship could not pull itself off. The ship was resting on her keel amidship and the relentless waves pounding the big ship caused her to rock on her keel and threatened to break her apart. Waves broke on the ship, their spray freezing on the ship.

They had no way to notify the Coast Guard of their peril, the ship was not equipped with a wireless radio. The captain knew the ship could easily be broken up by the waves and the crew would be killed by the waves, the rocks on shore, the debris thrown about by the seas or the cold. Their only option was to get off the ship before she broke into pieces.

Captain Recor asked for two men to row ashore and walk for help. The journey would be racked with danger. The odds were against them making it to shore through the storm tossed seas and the huge waves crashing on the rocks. Even if they made it, they would have to endure a freezing trek through deep snow in a blizzard. Two men, the first mate and one of the ship's wheelsmen volunteered.

The two men were lowered in the ship's yawl into the heaving sea. As the men struggled to row towards shore their boat was cast about by the waves,

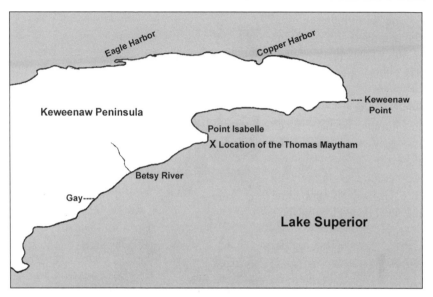

cakes of ice beat against their boat threatening to stove it in and the spray drenched the two men with freezing Lake Superior water. Nearing shore, the waves crashing on the rocky shore almost capsized the boat. Had the boat gone over the men would never have survived the waves crashing on the rocks or the frigid lake water.

The two men soaked and with icicles forming on their mustaches, jumped out of the boat before it was dashed on the rocks near shore. They struggled from exhaustion, exposure and fear as they fought off the pain of the freezing water and waded through the waves violently crashing on shore.

After what seemed an eternity, they made it to solid ground, but the solid ground was covered with snow drifts up to six feet deep!

The *Maytham* had gone hard aground on a reef off shore between Point Isabelle and the Betsy River on Upper Michigan's Keweenaw Peninsula. The area is densely wooded and sparsely populated. The two men thought their best chance of finding help was at the Betsy River where there was a year-round fishing village. They set off walking south towards the settlement at the Betsy River.

Wet through and freezing, the men struggled through the dense forest terrain in wind blown snow drifts sometimes deeper than they stood tall. The blizzard was blowing so hard most of the time the men couldn't see much beyond an arms length. They followed the shore, keeping the sound of the waves crashing on shore to their side.

The two men endured unimaginable hardships in their trek along the shore. The temperature was near zero and the gale force winds made the wind chill insufferable. Their legs felt as if they weighed a ton and their breath came hard but they continued on knowing that the lives of the men on the ship depended on their success.

They trudged though the deep snow for six miles before they came into the small fishing community.

At the Betsy River village, the men were warmed by a fire, given dry clothes, and hot coffee. But, there was no way to get news of the wrecked steamer to the Coast Guard from the village. The nearest telephone was in Gay, Michigan another seven miles distant.

A photograph taken as the crew left the Maytham *to the safety of the Coast Guard lifeboat. From the Edwin Brown collection of the State of Michigan Archives, Lansing, Michigan.*

The men thanked their hosts and took off again for the village of Gay. They set back off in the storm in a borrowed open fishing boat.

They hugged the shore, staying out just enough to avoid any shallows, boulders and the combers on the beach. The trip was another harrowing journey for the two brave men of the *Maytham*. Waves broke on their small boat and covered the men with a shower of spray. Their clothes froze to their skin and they re-grew their mustache icicles.

After a two hour trip in open water, the two heroic men arrived at Gay. The men were again taken in and fed and warmed by the residents while word was sent to the Eagle Harbor Coast Guard station of the stranded *Maytham* and the fear that the ship would be pounded to pieces by the vicious waves.

The Coast Guard station cutter was readied at once and departed into the wicked storm. Eagle River, located on the north side of the Keweenaw Peninsula meant the cutter had a 48-mile journey to get to the stranded steamer.

At the eastern point of the Keweenaw Peninsula the cutter came abreast to the west-southwest wind as they rounded the eastern end of the peninsula. Steaming between the narrow three mile wide pass between Keweenaw Point and Manitou Island, Captain E. W. Glaza, master of the Cutter, often found himself staring out at complete whiteness as the blizzard continued to rage.

The next course change around the peninsula brought the rescue vessel head-on into the storm.

The Coast Guard struggled through the wind threatening to blow them off course, the seas which crashed on their bow and pounded the ship relentlessly, and the blizzard which left them traveling blindly. But the men of the Eagle Harbor Station had a mission and they arrived near the *Maytham*.

They found the ship to be hard aground on the reef which extends out from Isabella Point. The *Maytham* rolled on its keel with each wave that crashed on the helpless ship. The storm had subsided a bit and it was decided the men must be removed from the ship immediately before the ship was reduced to pieces and the crew was cast into the freezing water to a certain death.

The lifeboat was lowered from the cutter and with careful and well practiced skills they were maneuvered to the lee of the ship. The crewmembers were waiting and anxious to risk the ride in a small boat to the safety of the Coast Guard cutter. It took several trips but all of the crew were removed from the violently rolling ship and safely transferred to the cutter.

An ice encased City of Bangor. *From the H.C. Inches collection of the Port Huron Museum.*

The deck cargo of the City of Bangor. *From the H.C. Inches collection of the Port Huron Museum.*

As the cutter pulled anchor and began to retrace her course to Eagle River the crew of the *Maytham* looked back at their ship. They took a long look knowing it would probably be the last they saw of the ship. The way she was rolling she would surely be destroyed by the lake.

Twelve miles into the return trip Captain Glaza, at the helm for the entire rescue, looked in disbelief as the cutter approached Keweenaw Point. There was another Great Lake steamer on the shore! The ship was covered in a thick layer of ice, like the *Maytham*, a victim of the storm.

The cutter maneuvered close to the frozen ship and the captain called to it with his megaphone. There was no response.

The Coast Guard lowered the yawl to send a crew to inspect the ship and search for survivors.

In its position on the eastern end of the peninsula, the west-southwest wind was blocked by the land and the seas were not quite as vicious as they were at the site of the *Maytham*.

The Coast Guard found the ship to be the *City of Bangor*, but there was no sign of her crew. The ship had been abandoned.

The Guardsmen reported back to the captain that the crew was missing, they theorized the crew must have left the ship fearing she was breaking up.

Captain Glaza ordered lookouts to scan the shore as they continued on through the storm. They hadn't gone far before movement was sighted in the forest. The crew, half frozen, was found on shore.

The Coast Guard shouted over the howling storm for the men to stay where they were. Captain Glaza assured them that they would return for them.

The cutter then headed to Copper Harbor, the closest port, where the crew of the *Maytham* was lodged in private residences, while the cutter returned to pick up the *Bangor's* crew.

The 445-foot long *City of Bangor* was another victim of the storm. Like the *Maytham*, the Bangor after 12 hours of being beaten up by the storm, had altered her course to seek shelter from the storm. The two ships independent of each other decided they had seen enough of the storm and came into the lee of the peninsula.

At 6:00 in the evening of Tuesday, November 30, 1926 the Bangor came to port in the blizzard, but her steam steering mechanism failed and they were left without a means to control the ship. Without steerage it wasn't long before the big freighter was thrown into the trough of the seas.

The *City of Bangor*, at the mercy of the sea, rolled mercilessly in the waves. A wave would crash down on her port side and she would roll, dipping

One of the damaged Chryslers from the City of Bangor. *Mounted on a sled for the trip to Copper Harbor. From the Edwin Brown collection of the State of Michigan Archives, Lansing, Michigan.*

her rail, then the big ship would roll back to starboard. There wasn't anything anyone aboard could do, but brace themselves and pray.

The *City of Bangor* was pushed into the shallows near the Keweenaw Point, abruptly stopping on the rocky shore. The ship, broadside to the beach rolled violently on its keel as the waves crashed down on the Bangor.

The waves came with such force that some of the chains holding the *Bangor's* deck cargo began to be ripped away. As the chains snapped, the cargo began to be tossed about on deck, some of the deck cargo was blown off into the surf to be battered on the rocks. The cargo the *City of Bangor* was transporting on that November 30th night... 248 brand new 1927 Chrysler automobiles. Eighteen of the Chryslers on deck had been blown overboard.

The master of the *City of Bangor*, knew his ship could not handle much more of the beating she was taking. The ship would soon start to buckle and break under the stresses it was receiving from the storm and Lake Superior.

Lake water, pouring in from every opening large and small, found its way to the engine room, but the pumps kept up with the inflow. The constant rolling of the ship on her keel, though, was too much and the hull cracked!

Cold Lake Superior water poured into the engine room through the cracked hull in torrents too great for the pumps to handle. The water rose and extinguished the boiler fires.

The wind and snow was so bad that when the *Maytham* sailed by the location of the Bangor, some 12 hours after the Bangor had grounded, no one from either ship saw the other. The huge Bangor was encased in a tomb of ice to make sighting it all the harder.

If the *City of Bangor* were to further break up, the crew would be cast into the wild surf. Any way the captain looked at it their only chance at survival was to get off the ship while they still could. He ordered the crew to abandon ship.

The crew of the Bangor took to the starboard side lifeboats and lowered down to the water. The starboard side lifeboats were used because they could be lowered behind the ship, away from the relentless crashing waves which would have beaten the port lifeboats to pieces.

Staying in the partially protected waters behind the Bangor, the crew in the lifeboats pulled for the shore. Through the grace of God and the skill of the men they all made it to shore without anyone killed or even injured.

The crew were cheered with their success. They had beaten the odds and gotten off the Bangor before it was broken into pieces, and they made it through the surf and stood on solid ground. But the captain knew the hardship they had so far suffered was about to become worse.

The cargo of brand new Chrysler automobiles from the City of Bangor *off loaded and awaiting the trip to Copper Harbor. From the H.C. Inches collection of the Port Huron Museum.*

The 29 members of the *Bangor's* crew now had to deal with the blizzard on shore, in a dense forest, in an area that rarely sees a man.

The men of the Bangor dug through the snow and gathered sticks to start a bonfire. Many of the crew had left the ship without warm clothing and now were freezing in the wind whipped blizzard. The crew knew they were in a precarious position, if they were not found soon or if they did not find shelter and food they would all freeze or starve to death.

They huddled around the fire by night and by day the officers and crew trudged though snow looking for a cabin or some type of shelter. After two days of this torturous journey the men were in a bad way. Many of the men were suffering from frostbite and the days of struggling through deep snow without any form of nourishment was leaving the men mentally and physically depleted.

The captain and officers tried to keep the crew's morale up and encouraged them to keep moving. They told the crew, to keep them moving, that there was a lighthouse nearby. The lighthouse was manned throughout the winter and they would find warmth and food there.

However, the only lighthouse in the area was miles away at Bete Grice Bay or another several miles in the other direction at Copper Harbor. The crew was not strong or healthy enough to make either.

A long line of Chrysler automobiles awaiting to be driven to Copper Harbor. From the Edwin Brown collection of the State of Michigan Archives, Lansing, Michigan.

The crew of the *City of Bangor* were never so happy to hear a voice when they heard Captain Glaza of the Coast Guard cutter call to them. The crew was disappointed that they would not be rescued immediately and that they would need to spend another night, the third, in the woods until Captain Glaza returned for them, but there wasn't room for both rescued crews on the cutter.

The crew of the *Maytham* was deposited at Copper Harbor and Captain Glaza and crew turned back into the storm to regain the marooned crew of the *City of Bangor*.

Despite all that Lake Superior could throw at them the crews of both ships lived through the ordeal. Several men were hospitalized with severe frostbite and suffering from exposure, but all lived to tell their tale.

The wrecking tug Favorite was called in to attempt to remove the *Maytham* from the shoal and eventually was able to pull the ship free before it froze in place for the winter. The Bangor was not as fortunate. An inspection revealed that the Bangor was too badly damaged and could not be moved.

The Bangor could not be removed but her cargo of brand new 1927 Chryslers needed to be taken off before the ship became encased in ice or broke up and destroyed the automobiles.

A ramp constructed of snow and ice was built to the ship's cargo hold and the cars were driven off of the ship. The Chryslers were driven across a make-shift winter ice road to Copper Harbor.

The two ships that slammed into the rocky shore of Michigan's Keweenaw Peninsula met with different results. The 30 year old *City of Bangor* was declared to be a loss and the hull was sold to salvager, T.L. Durocher. He attempted to remove her from the shore but the ship was found to be beyond repair and the *City of Bangor* was declared a constructive total loss. In 1942 the hull was cut up in place for scrap.

The *Thomas Maytham* was pulled free of the reef by the Soo wrecking tug Favorite and after $40,000.00 in repairs the *Maytham* once again sailed the Great Lakes. In 1935 the ship was converted to a tanker and renamed Dolomite 2.

In the year 1942 the ship was sold to Great Britain. On June 18, 1942 the *Thomas Maytham*, now re-named *Motorex* was torpedoed by a German submarine.

The *Maytham* that had spent years on the fresh water seas of the Great Lakes now lays for eternity in a saltwater grave. The broken hulk of the *City of Bangor* was scrapped for her steel to support the war effort, and the Chryslers were shipped back to Detroit for repair and resold.

SHIPS AT LEAST 400 FEET
PENOBSCOT

On October 29, 1951 there was an accident in the crowded harbor of Buffalo, New York. Three ships met and the result was a massive inferno that closed the harbor, destroyed two vessels, severely damaged another and killed eleven men.

The tragedy begins with tug *Dauntless No. 12* with the barge *Morania No. 130* in tow. The tanker barge towed by the tug took on a cargo of 800,000 gallons of gasoline at Cleveland harbor. The cargo's destination was Tonawanda, New York, some 180 miles distant.

The trip wasn't supposed to be anything out of the ordinary. The route the ships would follow would take them along the south shore of Lake Erie to Buffalo Harbor. There the tug and its tow would enter the Black Rock Canal and up to the Hambleton Terminal where the 800,000 gallons of gasoline would be discharged into shore tanks, just another routine run on the lakes.

The *Dauntless No. 12*, an 82-foot tugboat was owned and operated by the *Dauntless* Towing Line of New York City. The diesel driven vessel of 140 tons carried a nine-member crew including Captain Thomas Sorensen,

Penobscot   454 Feet in Length

The Great Lake Steamer, Penobscot. *Courtesy of the Lower Lakes Marine Society.*

George Van Steenburg, Mate, a chief engineer, an assistant engineer, two deckhands, a cook, and an oiler.

The barge, *Morania No. 130* of 1278 gross tons was 230-feet in length and was owned by Penn No. 5 Incorporated of New York, New York. Onboard the tanker *Morania* on that October day in 1951 was a crew of two, 29 year-old Captain Lars Stromsland and Mate Olav Gulleksen.

The barge was constructed so that when she was fully loaded most of her hull was under the water. She only showed three and a half feet of freeboard above the surface.

Captain Stromsland was anxious to get to Buffalo, his replacement was waiting there. The bargemen work twenty days on and then get ten days off. He was looking forward to his ten days ashore and out of the brisk October wind.

While enroute, the *Dauntless* and *Morania* were over run by a storm from the west. Since shallow Lake Erie kicks up rough in a storm, Captain Sorensen chose to shelter and ride out the storm.

The following day the storm broke and *Dauntless* and *Morania* were able to get under way. The *Morania*, towed several hundred feet behind the *Dauntless* on a thick steel towline, continued along the south shore of Lake

Erie on a northeast course. The course would take them to Buffalo harbor at the eastern end of the lake.

At approximately 11:00 PM, in the dark of night, the *Dauntless* and her barge slowed in preparation to enter the busy Buffalo Harbor.

After passing the Buffalo North Harbor Light, Captain Sorensen turned the tug into Buffalo's outer harbor. There in the protected waters behind the breakwater the forward motion of the barge was halted and the towline released. The crew on the *Dauntless* used the tow engine located at the aft of the tug to pull the towline aboard. After the towline was secured, the *Dauntless* made a wide circle around the barge coming to a position behind the barge to assume a pushing configuration.

The *Morania* was built with an inverted "V" in her stern. The purpose of the recessed stern on the barge was for the bow of the tug to fit into "V" shape.

The *Dauntless* slowly maneuvered behind the barge and into the "V" stern. Once fitted into the "V", the tug was secured to the barge with cables.

In the cramped confines of a harbor and river, the *Dauntless* would have much more control over its charge in a push arrangement than in the towing position. Rather than being a unit swinging at the end of a long line as when the two vessels were in the pulling arrangement, they were basically converted into one continuous unit.

Up the Buffalo River, the freighter *Penobscot* prepared to depart from the Mutual Elevator dock. The freighter had arrived in Buffalo the day before and off loaded its cargo of 200,000 bushels of grain. She now was preparing to depart.

The *Penobscot*, a 454-foot grain and automobile carrier owned by the Nicholson Transit Company of Ecorse, Michigan carried a crew of 30. The ship was one of the largest of the 14-ship Nicholson Transit Company's fleet.

The *Penobscot* had entered from Lake Erie moving upriver to the elevator, emptied her cargo and now had to be turned around to return to the lake. Two harbor tugs arrived to assist the freighter in turning.

Once all mooring lines were released from the dock, the tug's black smoke belching from their stacks pulled the freighter backwards to the turning basin where the large ship could be turned around. In the turning basin a tug gently nosed up to the *Penobscot's* bow to push the front of the large ship around until the she was facing downriver.

Captain Guyette blew a blast on the ship's whistle informing the tug to cast off the lines and soon the *Penobscot* was under her own power outbound towards the open water of Lake Erie. Their next stop was Detroit, Michigan where they would pick up a load of automobiles to deliver to Duluth, Minnesota.

The *Dauntless No. 12*, secured to the stern of the *Morania No. 130*, set a northwest course towards the Buffalo River entrance channel. The tug would cross the Buffalo River with the Coast Guard point on her starboard, proceed across the mouth of the river to the Erie Basin and on into the Black Rock Canal entrance channel. The two vessels would then travel up the Black Rock Canal to Tonawanda, New York to pump out her cargo of 800,000 gallons of gasoline.

The *Penobscot's* Captain, Louis Guyette, originally from Grindstone City, Michigan and now residing in the historic maritime river city of Port Huron, had been a sailor on the Great Lakes for 30 years, 20 years as a master with the last four as master of the *Penobscot*. His ship was leaving the Buffalo River and entering the Buffalo outer harbor and he knew it was a dangerous intersection, where it is difficult to see crossing ship traffic, especially in the dark. Captain Guyette looked out the port glass of the pilothouse and all he could see were the lights and buildings of the Coast Guard station.

"Keep a sharp eye out, Stan!", the captain shouted to Stanley Kielbasa, the third mate. Stan was the lookout on the deck at the bow.

When about 2000-feet from the spot where the river meets the outer harbor, wheelsman Richardson sounded one blast on the ship's whistle, a signal of warning when rounding a bend or any other maneuver where visibility was limited, to notify any ships of their presence and their intention of entering the outer harbor.

On the barge *Morania* there were only two crew members, Captain Lars Stromsland and his mate, Olav Gulleksen. Neither the captain nor his mate were forward standing watch at the bow of the barge as it entered the intersection. The barge entered the dangerous intersection of the Buffalo River and the outer Buffalo Harbor blindly.

Captain Sorensen onboard the *Dauntless*, eased his two ship unit to starboard past the Coast Guard base crossing the Buffalo River. He looked up the river but only saw the lights of the buildings along the river.

Even though it was dark, the barge did not display port or starboard, red or green, navigational lights at the bow, rather the lights were located aft. In 1951 according to Pilot Rules for Inland Waterways, barges being pushed by a tug only needed to display navigational lights towards the aft of the vessel, not at the bow, a rule which would be changed after the events of October 29, 1951.

The black, unlit bow of the barge *Morania* only 3 1/2-feet above the surface silently began to cross the river. The tug *Dauntless* displayed the necessary lights some 230-feet astern of the bow of the barge, but in the black of night the barge would be barley visible to other river traffic.

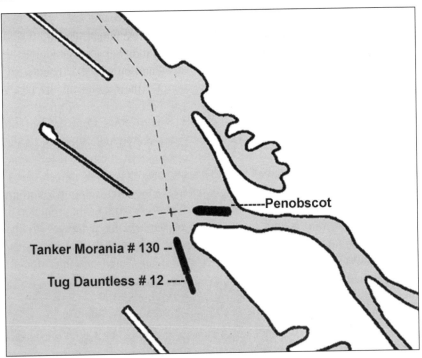

Tanker Morania # 130 --

Tug Dauntless # 12 ----

Penobscot

On the *Penobscot*, Third Mate Kielbasa and Able Body Seaman Albert Reid were in the windlass room at the bow. The tug had cast off the *Penobscot* and they were hauling in the tow line. They heard the captain blow the rounding bend whistle, and looked out forward. Stanley noticed something off their port quarter. As his eyes adjusted to the dark, he realized what it was.

"There's a ship crossing our bow!" he screamed.

Captain Guyette quickly assessed the situation and realized that a collision was possible and sounded the emergency danger signal, a long continuous blast, a sound that strikes fear in the minds of sailors, for it is a sound which all too often is followed by tragedy.

"Close all portholes and no smoking!" Captain Guyette's order sounded throughout the ship over the PA system.

All sailors knew that in a collision with a tanker the portholes were to be closed to keep the flammable cargo and fire from entering the ship. The no smoking order was for those aboard who did not know of the impending collision.

Captain Guyette threw the pilothouse telegraph to all astern full in an attempt to rapidly slow the forward momentum of the *Penobscot* and avoid ramming the barge.

Aboard the barge, Captain Lars Stromsland noticed the wind had freshened a bit and went out on the afterdeck. The barge silently moved through the water in the dark with lights of the city in the background, but the quiet of the night was blasted when the *Penobscot* sounded the danger signal. Captain Lars's head swung around to see the huge black hull of the freighter looming forward.

As the tug *Dauntless* rounded the Coast Guard point from the Buffalo outer harbor, Captain Sorensen was able to see the freighter outbound on the river. From the pilothouse of the tug the captain knew the bow of the barge was well into the river. He had to take evasive measures to avoid a collision. He couldn't stop in time and turning would take too long. Captain Sorensen thought his only option was to speed up and cross in front of the freighter.

Captain Sorensen sounded two blasts of the whistle indicating to the freighter he wanted to continue forward, passing in front of the freighter. Then the telegraph of the *Dauntless* clanged as Captain Sorenson called for all ahead full to give him the speed to cross in front of the *Penobscot*.

All of the evasive measures taken by the two ships were too late. The *Penobscot* in reverse had not yet slowed enough, the tug and barge could not gain enough speed to pass in front of the freighter, and the massive black bow of the *Penobscot* smashed into the barge about 30-feet from the barge's stern. The freighters bow was driven 3- to 4-feet into the starboard side of the barge bursting tanks numbers 5 and 6.

The gash in the side of the barge Morania *after the collision with the Penobscot. Courtesy of the Lower Lakes Marine Society.*

A fountain of gasoline three feet wide sprayed from the compressed and ruptured compartments, covering the *Dauntless*, the bow of the *Penobscot*, the deck of the barge and the surface of the river, in a shower of the volatile liquid.

Gasoline vapors filling the air permeated every compartment of the three ships and warned of an impending explosion.

Captain Guyette in the pilothouse filling with gasoline vapors, ordered the ship to be kept in reverse full. He had to get his ship away. The barge, spewing gasoline, was a time bomb waiting to explode.

The *Penobscot*, still in reverse, backed away from the barge, the steel hulls of the vessels scraping against each other in a gut wrenching screeching sound. The men on the ships held their breath, hoping the steel against steel of the hulls would not result in sparks.

Unfortunately their hopes were dashed as the two vessels grinding against one another ignited the gasoline vapors. In seconds the entire area was a mass of flames.

The abandon ship signal blasted throughout the *Penobscot*. The night sky was lit in an eerie orange glow as flames climbed to a height of fifty feet.

After hearing the danger signal blasting from the freighter, Captain Stromsland, aboard the barge, was knocked to the deck when his ship violently lunged to port as the two vessels struck.

He watched through the dark of night the huge outline of the *Penobscot* embedded in the starboard side of his barge. He could hear, see and smell the gasoline shooting from the gash in his ship. Then his worst nightmare was realized, the gasoline ignited. His ship was transformed into a world on fire. The entire area, the barge, the freighter, tug and water were ablaze.

"There was a flash and a flame and terrible heat all around," Captain Stromsland recounted.

The rush of heat instantly enveloped the captain. He pulled up his coat as he jumped off the burning ship, but the blast of intensely hot air burned his face and hands before he reached the water.

Captain Lars, admittedly not a strong swimmer, thrashed his arms and kicked in wild movements to get away from the burning barge which he knew was going to explode at any time and to escape the flames which leaped off the water.

The *Penobscot*, riding light without cargo, sat high in the water. Captain Guyette and Wheelsman Richardson high above the river's surface in the *Penobscot* pilothouse watched the gasoline ignite.

Flames climbed the gasoline soaked hull of the freighter consuming and igniting anything in its path. Following the gasoline vapors the flames roared

The Tanker barge Morania *after the fire. Courtesy of the Lower Lakes Marine Society.*

into the pilothouse instantly killing Captain Guyette and Wheelsman Richardson.

On the freighter, the 48 year old Second Mate Edward Homeier had just put on his pajamas and robe and was getting ready for bed. When he heard the long blast of the danger signal he quickly got dressed to see what was wrong. He first went to the windlass room and could smell gasoline.

"Don't anyone light a cigarette!" he yelled.

Almost as soon as he completed his sentence the ship was engulfed in flames.

Thomas Cree, a wheelsman on the *Penobscot* went off duty at 8:00 PM while the *Penobscot* was off loading its cargo of grain. He had a bite to eat and went to bed. Lying in his bunk he felt the ship being pulled to the turning basin by the tugs, heard the ship signal for the tugs to cast off, heard the warning bend signal, then he heard the startling blast of the danger signal.

Tom jumped out of bed, yelled to wake his roommate then looked out the porthole. Tom could see gasoline spraying from the barge.

As Tom looked in horror at the barge his view out the porthole became a vision of hell as the gasoline ignited.

Mr. Cree grabbed clothes and was dressing as another crewman, Francis Baker, came in yelling, "We're on fire!"

Smoke crept in from the door and hugged the ceiling of the room. The men huddled on the floor but it wasn't long before the smoke was too much for them and they knew to stay alive they would have to get out of the cabin and off the *Penobscot*. The three men crawled out the door into the passageway. Gasoline fueled flames climbed from the floor to the ceiling and they were blocked in each direction. They were trapped!

They saw another trapped crewman run and jump through the wall of flames. The three figured if he could do it they could too. Also, what other choice did they have. Each jumped into the flames only to land safely beyond the fire. They made their way to the main deck and crawled on hands and knees, burning both on the hot metal deck, up to the base of the forecastle.

Second Mate Homeier, the men from the windlass room, and men from the crew quarters ran aft away from the flames. The second mate left the group long enough to run down to the engine room. He found all of the engine room crew at their stations. He shouted, "Keep backing her!" to the Chief Engineer, David Binder. The second mate later said that he did not see the chief or his engine room crew abandon the burning ship.

The ship continued in reverse until it was clear of the burning gasoline covering the surface of the river. A lifeboat was lowered and about four or five crewmen scrambled aboard.

Dennis Smith assisted lowering the lifeboat but chose not to board it. "The fire on the water was still drifting towards us. I didn't want any part of being out there in a little boat." he later said.

The freighter, still full astern, backed away from the burning barge and tug. Still in reverse full the *Penobscot* smashed into the dock at the Coast Guard base. The impact with the dock shoved the rudder back into the propeller. The propeller was damaged, leaving the ship without propulsion or steerage.

Crewmen aboard the *Penobscot* could be seen running aft to escape the forward portion of the ship which was fully engulfed in flames. Some ran to the stern where watchman Ed Meyers tied a line to the rail, threw the rope over to waiting Coast Guardsmen who held the line taut while twelve crewmen slid down to the safety of the crumpled dock.

Flames shot from the freighter up into the lookout tower of the Coast Guard Station. "We're going to be burned out!" came an urgent call from the lookout, but the ship rebounded off the dock and floated back into the river, a 454-foot long torch drifting out of control in a busy congested harbor; a recipe for catastrophe.

The burned out hulk of the tug Dauntless. *Courtesy of the Lower Lakes Marine Society.*

Tom Cree and others were huddled on the deck by the forecastle until the drifting ship turned, blocking the wind which was keeping their small protected area free of smoke. As the smoke began to envelop them, the men had to find another area free of the choking smoke. They had to again jump through the flames to get to the other side of the ship where the smoke was blown away by the wind.

Two Patrolmen cruising the waterfront saw the flames and called in the fire. All available downtown firefighting apparatus were dispatched to the harbor including the fireboat *Grattan*. The *Grattan* directed its stream on the freighter, now a roaring inferno while a shore side fire truck played its searchlight on the scene.

Most of the remaining crew aboard the *Penobscot* were rescued by the fireboat *Grattan* and the tugs Ohio, California, and North Carolina, which dammed the flames and went to rescue the imperiled crew. Five members of the *Penobscot's* crew, all from the engine room were listed as missing.

Aboard the *Dauntless*, Captain Sorensen and his crew of seven did not have the option of backing away from the burning barge filled with 800,000 gallons of gasoline. They were physically cabled to it. The crews' only hope to escape the flames and possibly an explosion of the gasoline contained in the barge's intact tanks was to take to the water.

The captain and his mate jumped from the inferno into the burning water of the river and began swimming with all they had to escape the flames which encompassed everything. Captain Sorensen was wearing a life preserver but the mate was not. The mate swam along side the captain holding onto the life preserver belt.

Captain Lars Stromsland of the barge, swam for all he was worth to get away from the spreading flames. Not a strong swimmer, he made frantic moves, but he was weighed down by his clothing and shoes. Repeatedly sinking and swallowing water Captain Stromsland thought of untying his shoes and removing them but he was afraid if he stopped he might go under for the last time, so he continued struggling on.

Captain Sorensen and mate saw through the dense smoke and hellfire another person in the water making thrashing swimming moves trying to escape the conflagration. As the terrified person came closer Captain Sorensen recognized him. It was Lars Stromsland, captain of the *Morania No. 130*.

"Lars!" Captain Sorensen called.

Lars Stromsland had been frantically swimming away from the flaming barge for almost ten minutes and was nearing exhaustion when he heard a familiar voice and swam towards it with renewed vigor and hopes of salvation.

He saw that Captain Sorensen had a life jacket on and that George Van Steenburg was swimming along side holding onto the captain's life preserver with one hand.

The Penobscot *in drydock after the fire that killed the captain and wheelsman. Courtesy of the Lower Lakes Marine Society.*

Captain Stromsland commented, "I grabbed on to the other side. We kept swimming. I don't know when the mate slipped away, but suddenly he was gone."

"We sighted a small tug," the captain continued "and I had enough strength left to pull out a watertight flashlight I always carry in my hip pocket and signal with. They hauled me aboard with the tug captain and I collapsed on the deck. I don't think I could have made it many more strokes."

The Coast Guard lifeboats and the fireboat *Grattan* ignored their own safety and powered through walls of flames to rescue the unfortunate souls who needed to take to the water rather than remain on the ships and face certain death.

When the floating, flaming vessels drifted near shore, the firefighting apparatus on land pumped thousands of gallons of water on the ships.

Fire Commissioner Becker supervised the spraying of a fire retardant chemical from the deck of a Coast Guard vessel onto the tugboat *Dauntless*. By 1:30 AM the fire aboard the *Dauntless* was out.

Commissioner Becker boarded the smoldering tug and found one body in the wheelhouse. The body was burned beyond recognition.

"What an incinerator!" the commissioner said.

About the same time a Coast Guard surfboat went to the blackened hull of the barge. They were able to board the vessel, careful not to do anything which might ignite the remaining gasoline onboard.

Chief Boatswains Mate John Woldarek reported, "No signs of life."

"It's completely gone", he said. "Even the metal on the deck is melted."

The five men of the *Penobscot's* engine room crew that were missing and presumed dead were found to be below in the charred remains of the freighter. They had disregarded the abandon ship signal sounded and remained at their post backing the ship out of harm's way.

Seamen Dennis Smith praised the engine room crew for staying and keeping the burning ship running and backing out of the conflagration.

"The Old Man sounded the abandon ship several times but the engineers decided to stay aboard."

There were many people who did more than expected of them during the tragedy. The heroes included the Coast Guardsmen, the crew of the fireboat *Grattan* and the crews of the harbor tugs who ignored their own safety and plowed headlong into the flames to rescue the men on the burning vessels and in the water, and the fire fighters who battled the flames from their shore positions.

Other heroes included Francis Baker a member of the *Penobscot's* crew who took the time before he escaped the flaming ship to run throughout the ship waking his crewmates, many of whom were asleep when the catastrophe struck. The five men of the *Penobscot's* engine room who kept the freighter moving from the flames were also praised for their heroism.

The two men who received the most praise for their heroism were Captain Louis Guyette and Wheelsman Roy Richardson.

Survivor Albert Hayden said, "The credit goes to the captain. We wouldn't be here if the skipper hadn't put the freighter in reverse and headed it away from the fire. It was the skipper who gave the order to abandon ship and the wheelsman who stayed on his job, also should get a lot of credit."

David Niesley, a sixty-five year old survivor of the tragedy said, "The skipper and the helmsman saved us, but they paid for it."

Captain Stromsland, master of the tug *Dauntless No. 12* commented. "Apparently we did not see each other in time."

SHIPS AT LEAST 400 FEET
JAMES H. REED
AND THE
FRANK E. VIGOR

During World War II, President Franklin D. Roosevelt banned the production of civilian automobiles. The iron ore used to make steel that went into the manufacturing of the vehicles needed to be diverted to the building of weapons of war.

The automobile production facilities were re-tooled to make Jeeps, tanks, half track armored personnel carriers, airplanes and anything else the military needed, and civilian shipyards went into overtime building vessels of all types and sizes for military purposes.

The iron ore mined in Minnesota and upper Michigan was in demand. The military needed to insure its safe passage through the Great Lakes to the manufacturing facilities along the lakes. Because any disruption to the transport of the cargo would result in a delay in the construction and delivery of the weapons, the Army installed armed troops, searchlights, cannons and anti-aircraft units at the Soo Locks to guard against possible acts of sabotage.

Factories in Detroit turned out so many Jeeps, tanks and airplanes that it was nick named the "Arsenal of Democracy."

James H. Reed   455 Feet in Length

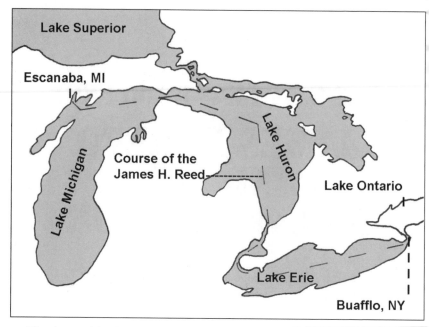

Lake Superior

Escanaba, MI

Lake Michigan

Course of the
James H. Reed

Lake Huron

Lake Ontario

Lake Erie

Buafflo, NY

The demand for iron ore was so great that just about any ship available was pressed into service to transport cargo. Even ships that were awaiting the wrecker were brought out of mothballs to run up the lakes to bring back iron ore so vital to the war effort.

The *James H. Reed* was one of the ships saved from the wreckers by the need for raw material. The *Reed* was built in 1903 but her forty one seasons on the lakes had taken a toll and advances in shipbuilding and navigation had passed her by.

In April 1944 the 455-foot *Reed* took on a cargo of iron ore at Escanaba, Michigan on northern Lake Michigan bound for Buffalo, New York on the eastern end of Lake Erie, a trip which would cover over 600 miles.

The passage took the ship from Escanaba through the Straits of Mackinaw and down the length of Lake Huron through the St. Clair River and Lake St. Clair. As the *Reed* steamed south through the Detroit River and approached Lake Erie she ran into a thick fog.

Captain Bert Brightstone, master of the *Reed*, knew the trip across Lake Erie would be slow and tedious. The *Reed* would need to check down her speed, sound the fog signal, and post lookouts to watch and listen for other ships in her vicinity.

The *James H. Reed* was not alone on the lake, there were other ships out on Lake Erie on that foggy April day of 1944. Some of them were the 546-

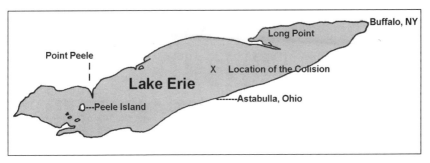

foot ore carrier *Ashcroft* which was heading to Toledo, Ohio, the east bound 412-foot *Frank Vigor*, the steamers *John Sherwin* and *Simalo* and the 480-foot *Philip Minch*.

The *Reed* slowly picked its way past the Detroit River lighthouse into Lake Erie. The ship's course would take it along the northern shore of Lake Erie to the narrow Peele Passage, between Point Peele and Peele Island. Captain Brightstone was particularly careful as the *Reed* crept along through the passage since it's less than 9 miles wide and all large ship traffic must pass through it.

The *Reed* navigated the passage and passed into the open water of the lake without incident. The ship was now clear to go the length of the lake to Buffalo.

At 5:08 in the morning the *James H. Reed* was creeping along in the fog about 42 miles west of Ontario's Long Point and 28 miles north of Ashtabula, Ohio. Suddenly the large iron ore carrier *Ashcroft*, one of the largest Canadian ships on the lakes, appeared out of the thick, pea soup fog. There was nothing either ship could do, the bow of the *Ashcroft* smashed into the port side of the *Reed* near hatch number 8.

The bow of the *Ashcroft* was badly damaged but she remained afloat. The *Reed* sustained damage to her hull that allowed the lake to pour in through the gash.

It was obvious the *Reed* would soon sink to the bottom of Lake Erie and the crew hurriedly went throughout the ship searching for their mates.

Within minutes the *Reed* sank in 60-feet of water. Twenty four crew of the *Reed* were picked up by the *Ashcroft*, which was standing by ready to render

Frank E. Vigor   412 Feet in Length

THE WEATHER
Light frost tonight in suburban areas; warmer Friday.
/ 8 Weather Bureau Forecasts
See MORE War Bonds and Stamps

The Detroit News

THE HOME NEWSPAPER FOR MORE THAN 90 YEARS

THURSDAY, APRIL 27, 1944, 71st Year, No. 240.   A Politically Independent Publication, Not Affiliated With Any Group of Newspapers.

Home Edition

FOUR CENTS

2 LAKE FREIGHTERS SINK IN CRASHES; 10 MEN LOST

any assistance she could. Unfortunately, twelve other crewmembers of the *James H. Reed* were carried down with the ship.

The survivors, several of them injured or suffering from exposure, were taken by the *Ashcroft* to Ashtabula, Ohio for medical treatment.

Just an hour after the collision of the *Ashcroft* and the *James H. Reed*, there was another incident on Lake Erie. In the narrow Peele Passage two other ships that had braved the dense fog came together in a disaster.

The shipping channel for large vessels takes the ships between Point Peele, an approximately 9 mile long peninsula that extends from the Canadian shore into Lake Erie, and Peele Island. The passage is less than 9 miles wide yet much of it is not of sufficient depth for large ship travel making the channel even narrower yet.

On the foggy morning of April 27, 1944 the 480-foot *Phillip Minch*, owned by the Kinsman Transit Company of Cleveland, Ohio, was traveling west in Lake Erie. On an easterly course to Buffalo, NY was the 412-foot steamer *Frank E. Vigor*. Both were near the narrow Peele Passage.

The *Vigor* was another of the older ships which was pressed into service to help with the war effort. The ship had been plying the Great Lakes since her launch in 1896!

10 Die, 2 Missing in Lake Disaster

Fog Results in Two Sinkings on Erie; Detroiter Among the Victims

The dense fog obscured the visibility of the ships as they crept along, sounding their fog signal and lookouts listening intently for other ships.

The captain, mate and helmsman on the bridge of the *Frank Vigor* were horrified when the bow of the *Minch* abruptly broke through the fog and rammed into the side of the *Vigor*.

The *Vigor*, holed below the waterline, began taking on water, almost instantly began to list and in short order the *Frank E. Vigor* rolled over and sank. The 30 men onboard jumped for their lives into the cold early spring Lake Erie water.

The *Minch* remained afloat and was not in danger of sinking. They quickly lowered their lifeboats and rowed towards the cries of the *Vigor's* crew. Once aboard the *Minch* many of the *Vigor's* crew were found to be suffering from exposure to the cold lake, none were seriously injured and all 30 had survived.

To meet the military's need for weapons of war almost any ship that could float was called into service to transport iron ore from the mines of Minnesota and Michigan to the industrialized cities around the Great Lakes. Two of the ships sailing the lakes to help meet the demand of the factories were the *James H. Reed* and the *Frank E. Vigor*. They both met with the same fate in foggy Lake Erie on the morning of April 27, 1944.

SHIPS AT LEAST 400 FEET
SIDNEY E. SMITH

Huge amounts of cargo are carried on the Great Lakes each season, coal, grain, iron ore, and stone being the principle commodities transported. If there is an interruption to the flow of the Great Lake ships, it could be disastrous to the region's and America's economy. An interruption to freighter traffic that halted the movement of the ships occurred in 1972 with the sinking of the *Sidney E. Smith.*

The purpose of a Great Lakes freighter is to carry cargo economically. To accomplish this, the ships must be of a size to carry a large cargo. The maximum size of the ship is only limited by the length and width of the locks at Sault Ste. Marie.

These mammoths of the lakes are in their element on the open waters of the Great Lakes, but they are cumbersome in the tight confines of harbors and rivers.

The St. Clair River is a little more than a half of a mile at its widest and less than a quarter of a mile as an average. It is the connecting waterway between Lake Huron and the St. Clair River. This narrow waterway is said to be one of the busiest on the lakes. Any commercial or recreational vessel

Sidney E. Smith   480 Feet in Length

The steamer Sidney E. Smith *passing through the St. Clair River. From the collection of the Port Huron Museum, Port Huron, Michigan.*

traveling between the upper lakes of Superior, Michigan and Huron and the lower lakes of Erie and Ontario must pass through the St. Clair River.

The fact that the total volume of Lake Huron empties into the river creating a tremendous current and the large amount of ship traffic on the river, it is easy to understand why the area has been the site of many maritime accidents. One ship that was a victim of the narrow St. Clair River, was the *Sidney E. Smith*.

The *Smith*, built in 1906 for the National Steamship Company, sailed under three names. She first sailed under the name *W. K. Bixby*, but when the 480-foot ship was sold to the Minnesota Transit Company in 1920 her name was changed to *J. L. Reiss*. Later the ship was named the *Sidney E. Smith*.

In September 1962, the 56 year old ship was still on the lakes and it was on the 23rd day of that month when the trusty ship had an "incident."

The Brockmiller family from Dearborn, Michigan was enjoying fall camping at the Algonac State Park located along the river. At 6:00 in the morning they laid in their sleeping bags listening to the ships passing on the river, sounding their whistles in an early morning fog.

Mr. Brockmiller said, "I could hear just the normal warning signals because of the fog. Then there was a series of quick short blasts, and a loud crunch."

At 6:00 AM the *J. L. Reiss* was up-bound on the St. Clair River with a load of coal. The ship was enshrouded in dense fog and the pilot was navigating by radar. Downbound on the St. Clair River at the same time was the 595-foot *Sewell Avery.*

About 150-feet from the American, (west) shore of the river, the two ships sideswiped each other. Both ships were damaged in the collision and quickly dropped their anchors.

The Sewell Avery. *From the collections of the Port Huron Museum.*

The *Avery* had a long scrape on its starboard side while the *Reiss* received the heaviest damage; about 60-feet behind the bow a two square foot section of steel was ripped out at the deckline.

Neither ship was seriously damaged or at risk of sinking. After a three hour delay, the *Avery* was permitted to continue south on its course. The *J. L. Reiss* remained anchored in the river awaiting a marine inspector.

Repairs were made to the *Reiss* and she was put back into service. For another ten years the freighter was a familiar sight on the Great Lakes.

In 1972, at an age of 66 years, the freighter was older than most of her crew. The *Reiss* was sold for the last time and again her name was changed.

Her new owners, the Erie Sand Steamship Company, re-named her *Sidney E. Smith Jr.* The ship had not operated under her new name for long when she suffered another "incident", and again it occurred on the St. Clair River.

The *Smith* was north bound with 4,000 tons of coal en route to Lime Island in the St. Marys River. The ship passed by the location where she sideswiped the *Sewell Avery* near Algonac and continued north in the St. Clair River.

At about 2:00 AM the crew in the pilothouse on the *Smith* watched the city lights pass by, Sarnia, Ontario on their starboard and Port Huron, Michigan on their port. Ahead the Blue Water Bridge was lighted with marker lights and the taillights and headlights of the trucks and cars crossing the international border.

In the pilothouse of the *Smith* that morning were Second Mate Henry Gaskins, and at the wheel was Paul Diehl. This was the first trip through the St. Clair River for Diehl and the first time Gaskins piloted the *Smith* on the river.

The weather that morning was almost ideal, no fog with temperatures in the mid 50's and the visibility was normal for 2:00 in the morning.

The radar on the *Smith* indicated another ship on Lake Huron on a southbound course preparing to enter the St. Clair River. On the clear night, the ship's lights could easily be seen in the distance.

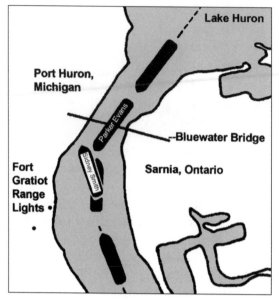

The southbound ship was the Parker Evans, a 530-foot freighter sailing under the Hindman Transportation Company flag. The Evans carried a cargo of 11,000 tons of grain loaded at Alpena, Michigan bound for Montreal, Quebec.

The Evans was on the recommended course for a southbound vessel entering the St. Clair River, lined up with the Fort Gratiot range lights.

At the bow of the *Smith* was Seaman Robert Shanahan, his duty that morning was the forward lookout while the ship passed through the busy St. Clair River.

Second Mate Gaskins told the wheelsman to come to the right slowly. He knew as they passed the Port Huron Water Works plant on the west side of the river, the ship had to be put to starboard in a long slow turn to make the river's bend and to keep the river's rapidly flowing current evenly on both sides of the ship.

About a half mile below the Bluewater Bridge, Mr. Gaskins noticed that the bow of the *Smith* seemed to be, "sagging towards the American shore."

"I noticed that the ship was not responding to the rudder, so I ordered hard right from the wheelsman," Gaskins said.

The wheelsman, Paul Diehl, held the wheel hard right.

Mr. Diehl later explained to the Inquiry Board; "I expected her to come about any time, but she didn't. By the time the mate hollered, "hard right," I had her as far as she would go."

The bow of the *Sidney E. Smith* continued to swing towards the west side of the river even though she was powering forward with her rudder to starboard. The river's tremendous current was pushing the *Sidney E. Smith* directly into the path of the oncoming freighter.

Five quick blasts came from the *Smith's* whistle to warn the other vessel.

At the bow of the *Smith*, Watchman Shanahan watched in horror as the large freighter bore down on his ship. He was prepared to lower the anchor but the order never came. Only once the collision was imminent did Shanahan leave his position. He was knocked from his feet as the Parker Evans rammed into the starboard side of the northbound *Sidney E. Smith* just feet from the forward lookout post. The hull of the *Smith* was ripped open, admitting tons of water into the gash.

Again the whistle of the *Sidney Smith* sounded, this time seven short blasts followed by two long ones; a signal for the crew to abandon ship.

Quick thinking Shanahan lowered the anchor right away. Then he ran for the crew quarters to awake the sleeping men.

That morning, Tom Harmon was on duty at the Lakes Pilot Association Office. He heard the ship's abandon ship whistle and ran to the window. From his vantage point he could see the two ships.

At the Sarnia Pilot's office, Captain Campbell heard the whistle blasts. He ran outside to see the two ships then ran in to call the Port Huron Coast Guard. The captain and Crewman William Chadwick boarded the 42-foot pilot boat and raced to the scene of the accident.

As the *Smith* began to take on a severe list to starboard, Mike Mahun, Naser Jihefe, and Jim Carmody launched the ship's workboat. They fought the legendary current of the river and rowed to shore. They looked for a line to use to secure the *Smith* to hold the ship in place.

When Captain Campbell arrived at the badly listing *Smith*, the crew were in the process of lowering a lifeboat. Rather than take to the lifeboat, the 31 men onboard scrambled down the rope ladder into the pilot boat. They were all taken to the Lakes Pilot Associations office.

An aerial view of the Sidney E. Smith *laying on the bottom of the St. Clair River after colliding with the Freighter Parker Evans. From the collections of the Port Huron Museum, Port Huron, Michigan.*

The Sidney Smith *lies in the river. From the collections of the Port Huron Museum.*

Only 20 minutes after being struck by the Parker Evans, the *Sidney E. Smith* rolled over on her side and settled to the bottom of the St. Clair River about 450 yards south of the Bluewater Bridge. About four feet of her hull remained above the surface.   The Evans immediately went to the American side of the river and tied up. It was not known how much damage she had received in the collision. Her bow was caved in but her pumps seemed to be keeping up with any incoming water.

The hull of the *Smith* was partially laying in the shipping channel. The Coast Guard immediately stopped all freighter traffic on the river. Their fear was that the hydrodynamic forces of a passing ship might dislodge the *Smith* and cause her to sink or move to a position where she completely blocked the river.

By daybreak 66 ships, 26 southbound and 40 heading north, were anchored in Lake Huron, in Lake St. Clair and in the St. Clair River waiting to pass through the river.

Thousands of tons of iron ore, coal and other cargo destined to ports all around the Great Lakes and some in route to overseas destinations were aboard the ships at anchor. If the river remained closed for a long period of time the maritime economy of the region would be drastically impaired.

The Coast Guard vessel *Acacia* placed a buoy north of the capsized hull of the *Smith*. The river was then opened on a very limited basis to allow the ships to pass. The river was opened first to the southbound ships. They had to travel very slowly past the wreck and were under the control and watchful eyes of the Port Huron Coast Guard. After a four hour period, the northbound ships were permitted to pass.

In the next days that followed, the hull of the 480-foot *Smith* developed a crack between the seventh and eight hatches. The crack, which continued to increase in size, was not caused by the collision. Divers verified that the stern section of the freighter was lying on the bottom where the depth is about 35-feet. The bow is over a section of the river which is 55-feet deep resulting in the bow not being supported. The weight of the bow section, the rivers current and the movement of the passing freighters were all causing the hull to crack.

When the crack was discovered, river traffic was again stopped. A reported 70 ships were anchored or docked throughout the Great Lakes waiting the reopening of the river.

The Coast Guard, governmental environmental organizations and downriver communities feared that the 49,000 gallons of bunker C fuel oil onboard the *Smith* might be released if the hull broke in two. It would cause thousands if not millions of dollars in environmental damage for as many as thirty miles downstream. The oil had to be removed.

Anchors were affixed to both the bow and stern of the *Smith* to hold her in place and hopefully prevent the hull from cracking more. The McQueen

A salvage barge and crane working on the wreck of the Sidney Smith. *From the Russell Sawyer Collection of the Port Huron Museum, Port Huron, Michigan.*

The pumping of fuel oil from the hull of the Smith. *From the collections of the Port Huron Museum.*

Salvage Company, using three tugs and two barges, began to pump out the fuel oil. Hampered by the ever present current and winds, the pumping process took several days, sometimes having to be halted by the weather.

The stern section of the Sidney Smith *moved out of the navigation channel. From the Russell Sawyer Collection of the Port Huron Museum, Port Huron, Michigan.*

On June 12, 1972, seven days after the collision, the *Sidney E. Smith* split in two. In spite of three 4,500 pound Navy type anchors holding it in place, the bow shifted and broke off the stern section.

The owners of the *Smith* took bids for the salvage of the wrecked vessel. Since it had been broken apart there was no thought of repairing the ship. The vessel was only good for her scrap value.

The hulk of the broken vessel was removed from the river. The bow section was dismantled and the larger stern section was towed to the Canadian side of the river to be sunk in place as part of a dock.

The 480-foot *W. K. Bixby, / J. L. Reiss / Sidney E. Smith* met its demise on June 5, 1972, sixty six years after her launch. The crew of 34 aboard the *Smith* at the time of the collision, were removed from her safely.

Billy Minola, a crew member on the *Smith* still in good humor after the capsizing of his ship said, "...I probably had the shortest run on this ship of anyone."

Minola had first boarded the *Sidney E. Smith* at the Ambassador Bridge crossing the Detroit River. Four hours later, he got off the *Smith* at the Bluewater Bridge, crossing the St. Clair River. However he departed the ship not quite as he had planned.

SHIPS AT LEAST 500 FEET
S.S. PIONEER

In 1846, just two years after iron ore was discovered in the Marquette Range of Michigan's Upper Peninsula, the Cleveland Iron Mining Company was formed to mine and transport iron ore to the steel mills around the Great Lakes.

Throughout the years, the Cleveland-Cliffs Inc. acquired and merged with many small and large companies eventually obtaining large tracts of land for mining and forestry operations and an extensive fleet of ships to transport the iron ore mined in northern Michigan and Minnesota.

One ship in the Cleveland Cliffs Company's fleet was the *S. S. Pioneer*. The *Pioneer* was 504-feet in length by 54-feet in beam. Built in Wyandotte, Michigan in 1907, the ship carried millions of tons of iron ore from the ore docks on Lake Superior to the mills on Lakes Michigan and Erie and the Detroit River.

On the morning of September 30, 1953 the *Pioneer* departed Superior, Wisconsin with over 9,000 tons of iron ore bound for Lake Erie. The captain of the *Pioneer* would not learn the exact location until the company determined which mill was most in need.

Pioneer   504 Feet in Length

The 504-foot Pioneer. *From the collections of the Port Huron Museum.*

The *Pioneer* steamed across Lake Superior to the locks at Sault Ste. Marie, Ontario and Sault Ste. Marie, Michigan where the ship entered a lock at the level of Lake Superior and exited the lock 22-feet lower at the level of the St. Marys River. The ship maneuvered down river passing into the northern end of Lake Huron.

Lake Huron was clear sailing for a ship the size of the *Pioneer*. The ship could steam at full speed on the recommended down-bound course to the foot of the lake where it empties into the St. Clair River.

The St. Clair River is a 37-mile long connecting waterway between Lake Huron to the north and Lake St. Clair to the south. Any ship traveling between the upper lakes of Superior, Michigan or Huron and the lower lakes of Ontario and Erie must pass through the St. Clair River.

The river, less than a mile at its widest point, is a ship watcher's delight. All sorts of vessels pass by, ranging from recreational boats, both power and sail, to Great Lakes freighters of all sizes and foreign ships that entered the Great Lakes through the St. Lawrence Seaway.

The St. Clair River is an international border separating Ontario, Canada on its eastern bank and on the west bank is Michigan of the United States.

As the *Pioneer* moved south in the channel, Captain O'Leary could see the headlights and taillights of the vehicles crossing the Bluewater Bridge.

The 6,178-foot long Bluewater Bridge rises 152-feet above the river connecting Sarnia, Ontario and Port Huron, Michigan.

About 10:30 PM on October 2, 1953 the *Pioneer* passed the Huron Lightship anchored at the southern end of Lake Huron warning ships of the shallow Corsica Shoal. Captain O'Leary was piloting his vessel on the Point Edward Range Lights in the approach channel to the St. Clair River.

S.S. PIONEER

The weather in the Sarnia-Port Huron area was calm and clear, nothing but the dark of night to hamper visibility.

Up-bound on the St. Clair River that evening was the 205-foot *Wallschiff*. The *Wallschiff* was a brand new German freighter having only been launched two months earlier.

The trip for the *Wallschiff* and its crew began in Antwerp, Belgium where she took on a cargo of steel beams bound for Montreal, Toronto, Cleveland and Detroit. After crossing the Atlantic Ocean the ship entered the St. Lawrence Seaway and made the ports delivering and taking on cargo. On October 2, the *Wallschiff* departed Detroit after taking on 325 metric tons of sheet metal bound to Muskegon, Michigan on Lake Michigan. The ship powered up the Detroit River and crossed the length of Lake St. Clair where she entered the St. Clair River on her way to Lake Huron.

Onboard the *Wallschiff* were Captain Nessen, master of the ship, Captain Harold Patterson, a licensed Great Lakes pilot, the crew of 15 and one passenger. The ship entered the St. Clair River and maneuvered upriver towards the Bluewater Bridge.

Captain O'Leary was on the *Pioneer* heading south, entered the river and as it passed under the Bluewater Bridge he saw an up-bound ship several

The locks at Sault Ste. Marie. From the collections of the Port Huron Museum.

hundred feet south of the bridge. The oncoming ship, the German *Wallschiff*, seemed to Captain O'Leary to be much too close to the west bank of the river than a northbound ship should be.

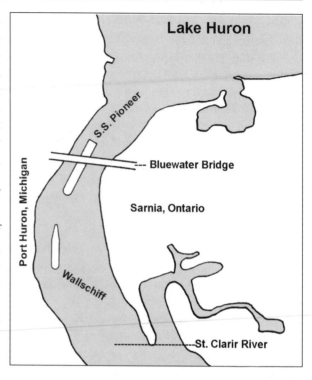

The captain of the *Pioneer* upon seeing the *Wallschiff* too far to the west, sounded his whistle twice, indicating his desire for a starboard-to-starboard passing. Normally ships would pass on one whistle or port-to-port in this area of the river. But the *Wallschiff* was too far to the west, or towards the American side, to allow for a port side passing.

As the 504-foot long *Pioneer* steamed south at 11 miles per hour preparing to pass the *Wallschiff* on her starboard side, Captain O'Leary told the helmsman, "Left some more" to allow more room for the passing. Not hearing an answering signal from the *Wallschiff*, Captain O'Leary sounded a danger whistle and rang the general alarm as a precaution, then shouted to the helmsman, "Hard Left!" As he watched, the German ship came to the right crossing the path of the *Pioneer*.

About 600-feet south of the Bluewater Bridge, despite taking evasive measures, the bow of the *Pioneer* smashed into the port side of the German freighter.

The *Wallschiff* was holed above and below the waterline and water poured in. The ship took on a list and began to sink.

Of the 16 man crew all but four were asleep. As the ship began to sink a 15 year-old deckhand, Heinz-Werner Schulz ran from the bridge where he had been the wheelsman during the collision to wake the others.

In the engine room, Frederich Peterson, the chief engineer of the *Wallschiff* was thrown about 8-feet when the *Pioneer* rammed into the side of the German ship. As the ship took on a sharp list with water rushing into the engine room, the engineer quickly scrambled to his feet, turned on lights and started the pumps. The pumps were running but the water kept rising. Mr. Peterson and his assistant raced up to the deck. Seeing the ship was about to slip beneath the surface, they jumped in the river and were rescued by the *J.W. Westcott* Marine reporting launch that was on the river.

On deck the crew were in a state of panic. Two men jumped from the ship and began swimming towards the Canadian shore. One man jumped in and swam to the *Pioneer* which had anchored nearby.

Several of the *Wallschiff* crew were trying to launch the ship's lifeboat but could not because the davits were stuck. Just as the water reached the deck the lifeboat swung free and the men climbed aboard.

Harold Patterson, the Canadian Great Lakes pilot, was seen running for his stateroom just after the collision. His lifeless body was later found floating in the river. He had suffered a fatal heart attack.

As the *Westcott* was returning to shore with the two men they pulled from the river, they heard a man screaming. They looked about and saw Captain Nissen. The captain had climbed up the masts as the ship sunk to the bottom in 40-feet of water.

The next day the riverbank was packed with people looking at the location of the sunken ship. All that could be seen were the ship's masts rising out of the water. The ship did not pose a hindrance to navigation but the Coast Guard posted red lanterns on the masts and requested that passing ships go by the *Wallschiff* slowly.

Not all collisions occur during thick fog or blinding snowstorms. The collision between the German *Wallschiff* and the *S.S. Pioneer* happened on a clear night, but pilot error can be just as deadly.

SHIPS AT LEAST 500 FEET
J.F. SCHOELLKOPF JR.

A look at a map of Lake Superior reveals the Keweenaw Peninsula as the most prominent feature of the lake. Ships traveling the southern shore of Lake Superior from the Soo Locks toward Duluth, Minnesota, or in reverse, would have to head north around the peninsula then head south, but ships can cut over 100 miles off the trip by cutting across the Keweenaw Peninsula through the Portage Canal Ship Canal.

The canal was completed in 1874 by blasting out a 2 mile long, 100-foot wide, and 14-foot deep waterway through the rock connecting Lake Superior at the west and Portage lake on the east side of the peninsula. The Portage River leading from Portage Lake to Lake Superior was then widened and deepened to complete the canal.

Along the canal are two major Upper Peninsula cities, on the south side is the city of Houghton, Michigan and on the north is Hancock, Michigan. In 1875 a swing bridge was built across the canal to connect the two cities. The bridge was built with two levels, the lower for railroad traffic and the upper for street traffic.

When a ship approached the bridge they blew the signal to open, 4 blasts on the steam whistle. The Bridge Engineer would then turn the wheel which

J.F. Schoellkopf Jr.   557 Feet in Length

The 557-foot J.F. Schoellkopf Jr. *From the Hugh Clark Great Lakes Collection.*

released the latch which held the span in position. The bridge would pivot on its center piling creating an opening for the ship to pass through.

By 1959 the old swing bridge was showing wear. It was deemed necessary by State maritime and highway officials that a new bridge needed to be built to accommodate larger the ships which were plying the Lakes and the automobile and truck traffic.

State of Michigan engineers made a study and recommended that a vertical lift bridge would be the best form of conveyance across the river.

The Houghton vertical lift bridge was completed and opened in December of 1959 with the dedication celebration of the new bridge scheduled for June 25, 1960.

The celebration was going to be a huge event. High school bands would play. Politicians would be there for photo opportunities and even a fly-over by the United States Air Force was scheduled.

The day before the dedication celebration, the 557-foot, 53 year-old Great Lakes freighter *J.F. Schoellkopf Jr.* was on the canal approaching the new lift bridge.

Following proper protocol, Captain Wilhelmy of the *J.F. Schoellkopf Jr.* sounded the whistle signaling the bridge to open. The ship proceeded on towards the bridge. The captain watched to see the bridge open but it didn't. Possibly the bridge operator was waiting for traffic to clear before the blinking red lights were turned on and the gates closed.

The captain and wheelsman watched intently for the bridge to begin the opening process. A Great Lakes freighter requires miles to stop. Stopping and waiting for the bridge to open was not an option. The bridge had better open soon.

A photograph of the original Portage Ship Canal. From the collection of Chuck Voelker, CopperCountryReflections@pasty.com.

Additional soundings on the whistle did not result in the bridge opening. Maybe they are having troubles, thought the captain. Captain Wilhelmy knew he had better take measures.

"Reverse full!" came the order.

The captain knew it was necessary to stop the forward momentum of the ship. If not his ship would crash into the brand new $11 million Houghton vertical lift bridge, and on the day before its Grand Opening celebration.

Construction of the new vertical lift bridge across the Portage Ship Canal. Courtesy of the Houghton County Historical Socity.

Captain Wilhelmy watched out the windows of the pilothouse. The bridge was not rising, nor did it appear that there was any attempt to open the bridge. There were no bells, no flashing lights, no road traffic barricades lowered, pedestrians and automobile traffic continued across the span.

A collision between the steel bridge and the *J.F. Schoellkopf Jr.*, even with the ship at a reduced speed and in reverse would be catastrophic. In a best case scenario the roadbed of the bridge would be bent and broken and the bow of the ship would be damaged.

In the worst case the roadbed would be ripped from its two supporting towers and pushed into the waterway, the towers would be pulled from their foundations and crash into the canal on top of the roadbed. The bridge would be destroyed and the waterway blocked by the debris, leaving the canal un-navigable for months.

The loss of life could be extensive as the pedestrian and automobile traffic, not stopped by barricades, drove off the bridge into the water below.

Damage to the *J.F. Schoellkopf Jr.* had the potential to be devastating as well. The *J.F. Schoellkopf Jr.*, being a ship of its era, was constructed with the pilothouse at the bow, unlike the modern Great Lake freighters that are piloted from the stern.

A collision with the Houghton vertical lift bridge could severely damage the forward structure leaving the 53 year-old vessel too expensive to repair. The once proud *J.F. Schoellkopf Jr.* would probably finish out its usefulness on the lakes as a barge, as a floating storage container or it would be towed to the salvage yard to be scrapped.

Captain Wilhelmy watched the bridge as his ship bore down on it. The order to reverse had slowed the ship but still a collision was immanent.

"Lower the anchors!" Captain Wilhelmy shouted to a deckhand standing at the ready.

The anchors splashed into the canal and the heavy chain roared as it was payed out.

The anchors dragged along the bottom, the *J.F. Schoellkopf Jr.* continued forward towards the bridge. Suddenly the anchor chain snapped taut. The anchors held fast to the bottom and stopped the ship, averting what could have been a major maritime disaster.

The quick thinking and actions of the captain were responsible for preventing the collision. He responded by reversing the engine and dropping the anchors. The anchors dragged until the hooks snagged two submarine telephone cables traversing the Portage canal.

The J.F. Schoelkopf Jr. *with it's prow under the Zilwaukee Bridge.*
Courtesy of the State of Michigan Archive. Lansing, Michigan.

The Grand Opening celebration took place the following day. Many of those attending were not even aware of the near tragedy of the day before. But there were those who were well aware of the incident; the hundreds without telephone service and the bridge operator who said, he simply didn't hear the ship's whistle.

During the late 1950's the United States government developed the Interstate Highway System to allow for high-speed express travel on limited access roads. I-75, the multiple lane expressway, traverses north and south from the Canadian boarder at Sault St. Marie, Michigan over one thousand six hundred miles to Miami, Florida.

A person could conceivably drive from one of the most northern points in the United States to one of the most southern without ever stopping.

A double leaf bascule bridge, or more commonly known as a draw bridge, was built to carry the I-75 highway traffic over the Saginaw River.

On October 5, 1967 a Great Lakes freighter *J.F. Schoellkopf Jr.* was carefully threading its way along the Saginaw River from Lake Huron's Saginaw Bay. It navigated the curving river with its four bascule bridges and two railroad swing bridges. The ship discharged its cargo of limestone upriver and began its return voyage downriver to the open water of Lake Huron's Saginaw Bay.

As the ship approached the draw bridge at Zilwaukee, which carried the cars and trucks of I-75 over the river, the steering mechanism of the ship failed! The ship attempted to slow and stop but it just wasn't going to happen.

The *J.F. Schoellkopf Jr.*, the ship that avoided colliding with the Houghton vertical lift bridge, crashed into one of the columns supporting the southbound lanes of the I-75 expressway. The ship, traveling at a slow speed, received very little damage and fortunately the damage to the bridge was also minimal and the traffic was diverted from the southbound lanes for several days while the damage was analyzed and repaired.

SHIPS AT LEAST 500 FEET
J.P.
MORGAN JR.

Prior to the advent of weather computer programs and Doppler Radar, Great Lake's sailors had little in the way of weather forecasting. They would study the sky and make an educated guess but often the weather conditions when leaving port were not the conditions the ship would experience en-route. Storms would blow in un-expectantly, temperatures might drop to freezing during the night on a beautiful fall day, but the condition that caused the greatest concern for Great Lakes sailors was fog.

The big ships could handle the wind, waves and thunder storms but being blinded in a fog could cause mammoth steel freighters to lay dead in the water waiting for visibility to improve.

When encountering fog or other conditions which cause reduced visibility, Great Lakes ships are required to sound a fog signal and check down their speed to a rate that would allow the ship to come to a complete stop in the distance they could see.

On the morning of Wednesday June 23, 1948 The 580-foot Pittsburgh Steamship Company's steamer *J. P. Morgan Jr.* was underway in a thick summer fog.

J.P. Morgan Jr.   580 Feet in Length

Launching the J. P. Morgan, Lorain, Ohio.

The J.P. Morgan *at her launch. From the collection of William Forsythe and David Huskins.*

The *J. P. Morgan Jr.* had taken on 12,800 tons of iron ore at Duluth, Minnesota to be delivered to a steel mill in Cleveland, Ohio. The trip would take the ship west to east across Lake Superior, through the Soo Locks, down the length of Lake Huron, through the St. Clair River, Lake St. Clair and the Detroit River and 80 miles across Lake Erie. This was a trip the ship and crew were familiar with, having done it several times already during that 1948 season

Sixty year-old John Pekkala, a wheelsman aboard the *Morgan*, had worked the lakes most of his life, the last four years he served on the *Morgan*. He was relieved of his watch, ate quickly and went to his berth at the forward port quarter. Also

Lake Superior

X Approximate Location of the collision

Keweenaw Peninsula

The Crete. *From the collections of the Port Huron Museum.*

getting off watch was 18-year-old Duane Strand from Willmar, Minnesota. Deckhand Strand was in his cabin at the forward port quarter of the ship sleeping through the blasting of the fog signal.

The *Morgan* was not equipped with radar and relied on the eyes and ears of its lookouts posted about the ship to provide an early warning of any other ship in their vicinity during periods of reduced visibility.

The fog which was enveloping the area ranged from as much as 2 ° miles to a low of 1000-feet.

At 3:45 AM, the first mate of the *Morgan*, Richard Grant, assumed the bridge of the *Morgan*. The ship was following the Great Lakes Association recommended down-bound course between Devils Island and Eagle Harbor on Michigan's Keweenaw Peninsula.

The mate noted that the ship's engine room telegraph was set for full speed and making about 11 miles per hour. It was recorded in the ship's log that they encountered fog of varying densities, from visibility of up to 2-1/2 miles to less than 1000-feet.

At 5:48 AM the mate overheard a radio conversation between two ships. The *Crete* and the *J. C. Wallace* discussed weather conditions and their positions. The *Crete* said they were up-bound on a course between Jackfish Bay, Ontario and Devil's Island.

When the mate recorded their position, 30 miles northeast of the Portage Ship Canal, he also made note of the fact that the *Crete* was in their area but not on a course that would cause the two ships to cross.

The damaged pilothouse of the J.P. Morgan. *From the collection of the Bayliss Library, Sault Ste. Marie, Michigan.*

The *Crete*, with the Interlake Picklands Mather Fleet, was running across Lake Superior to load at Duluth.

About eight minutes later, the *Crete* established another radio communication with the *Wallace* to inform them that they had made a course change in order to cross the down-bound shipping lane.

Hearing the broadcast, the mate on the *Morgan* sent a lookout to wake the captain. Captain Quinn had left a standing order to be called in the event of any trouble.

There is old ship masters adage that says: "If you wake me and it's nothing, I will go back to sleep. If you do not wake me and it's something, I will never be able to sleep with you on duty."

When the captain entered the bridge, First Mate Grant told Captain Quinn of the two radio transmissions from the *Crete* and *Wallace*. The captain ordered the lookouts to keep a sharp eye, and to report any fog signals. He then, at 6:09 AM made a radio call to the captain of the *Crete*.

The two captains conversed about conditions and Captain Quinn requested a one-whistle passing, meaning the two ships would pass port-to-port. The captain of the *Crete* did not agree or disagree with the passing arrangements.

Three minutes later the *Crete* called the *Morgan* and said they could not make a one-whistle passing and preferred a two-whistle passing (starboard-to-starboard)

As they talked, the fog whistle of the *Crete* could be heard in the pilothouse of the *J. P. Morgan. Jr.* Upon hearing the signal, Mate Grant sounded the danger signal to alert the other ship and the *Morgan's* crew.

The fog signal told Captain Quinn the *Crete* was closer than he thought and immediately rang "Standby" on the ship's Chadburn.

The order would stop the engines but not stop the ship. A 580-foot long steel ship running at full speed takes several miles to come to a full stop. The *Morgan* was still gliding forward from momentum. The captain ordered the helmsman to turn a bit to the left. In case the ships came close enough to touch, it would be a glancing blow, which would cause less damage than a straight on collision.

The pilothouse crew and lookouts could hear the fog signal of the *Crete* coming closer off their port bow somewhere in the thick white fog. Captain

The J. P. Morgan *being towed through the St. Clair River. The temporary patch on the hull can be seen. From the Russell Sawyer Collection of the Port Huron Museum, Port Huron, Michigan.*

Damage as seen from the port aft. From the Russell Sawyer Collection of the Port Huron Museum, Port Huron, Michigan.

Quinn ordered the ship to full speed astern to stop the forward motion of the *Morgan*.

Within a minute, the huge bow of the *Crete* appeared through the veil of fog off the *Morgan's* port bow. The *Crete* was approaching the *Morgan* at almost a 90 degree angle. The wheel on the *Morgan* was turned hard to starboard and the propellers were churning up white foam but there was no stopping the ships. The bow of the *Crete* tore into the port side of the *Morgan* at the forecastle, ripping a hole from the bottom plates up to the pilothouse. The forward bulkhead was breached and lake water poured in, flooding all forward compartments.

The crew in the pilothouse at the time of the collision were thrown to the deck and nearly crushed as the bow of the *Crete* drove deep into the superstructure of the *Morgan* leaving the bridge suspended above the wreckage.

Captain Quinn saw the severe damage his ship had sustained; fearing it wouldn't remain on the surface long he ordered the crew to abandon ship.

In the tradition of the lakes, Captain Quinn remained on his ship, vowing to be the last to leave the *J. P. Morgan Jr.*

A radio call was sent out and received by the United States Coast Guard Cutter *Woodrush* moored at the Portage Ship Canal some 30 miles distant. The Coast Guard then notified the Army Corp of Engineers to ready their tugboat *Barlow* to respond the to the crash scene.

Another ship in the vicinity of the collision of the *Crete* and the *Morgan* was the 622-foot Pittsburgh Steamship Company's *Voorhees*. Ships on the Great Lakes have an unwritten vow to help others when in need, for you never know when you might need their help. The *Voorhees* steamed, with caution, to the scene to render any assistance they could.

The *Morgan's* hull was breached from the keel to the bridge, with water pouring into the gash yet the ship did not sink! She was severely damaged but remained afloat.

Seeing the *Morgan* was not sinking, the crew boarded the ship and began to survey the damaged area.

On Great Lake freighters there are two watertight bulkheads, or walls, which rise from the keel up to the spar deck and across the breadth of the ship. The most forward is called the collision bulkhead. In case of a head on collision with another ship or some structure, the collision bulkhead is designed to hold the incoming water from getting further aft in the ship. A second bulkhead is located at the forward end of the cargo hold.

The J.P. Morgan *damaged pilothouse. From the Russell Sawyer Collection of the Port Huron Museum, Port Huron, Michigan.*

In the collision of the *Crete* and the *J. P. Morgan Jr.*, the damage to the *Morgan* was not bow on; rather the *Morgan* was struck at a 90 degree angle. The impact damaged the *Morgan's* collision bulkhead allowing water to flood the forward compartment back to the forward cargo bulkhead.

The *Crete* struck the *Morgan* straight on with very minor damage, its collision bulkhead remained intact. The *Crete* was not in any danger of sinking and stood by to take on survivors of the *Morgan* if needed

Aboard the *Morgan* several men had been injured during the collision. The impact had sent the crew hurling through the air. Some smashed into equipment or were thrown to the deck. A wheelsman had lacerations and several broken bones in his hand, a deckhand had chest injuries and the second mate had broken his hip.

But In the forward port quarter of the *J. P. Morgan Jr.* where the damage was greatest, two men who had been relieved of their duty and gone to sleep in their cabins, John Pekkala and Duane Strand, were killed instantly when the bow of the *Crete* smashed into the hull of the *J. P. Morgan Jr.*

The *Morgan* moved to the Portage Ship Canal. Since her pilothouse was destroyed she had no ability to steer, but the tug *Barlow* provided steerage and the *Morgan* was able to travel under her own power.

In the investigation that followed, during the time of the collision Captain Quinn was found to be guilty of misconduct by violating Great Lakes Rule # 15.

Specifically the Great Lakes Rule 15 states:

"Every vessel shall, in thick weather, by reason of fog, mist, falling snow, heavy rain storms, or other causes, go at a moderate speed. A steam vessel hearing, apparently not from more than four points from right ahead, the fog signal of another vessel shall at once reduce her speed to bare steerageway, and navigate with caution until the vessels shall have passed each other."

The captain's license was suspended for two years, one year outright and the second year on probation. The captain appealed the decision and due to his good past record his license was suspended for a period of one year, the first two months outright and the last ten months on probation.

Captain Quinn retained his license and the two ships were eventually repaired and put back into service on the Great Lakes, but two men were killed and several others were injured in the collision of the *J. P. Morgan Jr.* and the *Crete*.

SHIPS AT LEAST 500 FEET
WILLIAM C. MORELAND

On July 27, 1910 the big steamer *William C. Moreland* slid down the ways of the American Shipbuilding Company to start her career of carrying iron ore from the mines of the upper Midwest to the steel furnaces of the lower lakes.

The brand new ship was fitted out and her first trip was in September of 1910. Her owners were anxious to recoup the $450,000.00 cost of building the ship, and start making a profit.

The *Moreland* measured 580-feet in length with a gross tonnage of 8,800 tons. The ship fell into the routine of loading iron ore from Duluth and Marquette and delivering it to the steel mills along Lake Erie. The ship, since it was big and new, was a favorite to see passing through the locks and the St. Clair and Detroit Rivers.

On the fifth trip of its existence, the large ship had taken on a cargo at Superior, Wisconsin and cleared the dock early in the morning of October 18, 1910.

Captain Ennes set a northeast course for the ship that would take her out from the harbor and across the top of the Keweenaw Peninsula, the *Moreland* was much too large to use the Portage canal. Once rounding the peninsula, a

William C. Moreland 580 Feet in Length

The William C. Moreland *grounded and ice covered. From the State of Michigan Archives. Lansing, Michigan.*

course change to southeast would be made taking the vessel to the locks at the Soo, then down Lake Huron arriving in Lake Erie to off load the ore. It was nothing out of the ordinary, just another routine trip.

The ship's passage should take it about 1-1/2 to 2 miles off the rocky coast of the Keweenaw. That course would provide more than enough water under her keel.

On that day in mid October, there was another event occurring that would impact the big *William C. Moreland*, this one on land.

In the early 1900's the vast forests of the upper Midwest supplied millions of board feet of lumber to meet the needs of the growing populations of the urban areas. The method that was employed by the lumbermen was to cut down a tree, de-limb it and cut the trunk into manageable lengths.

The limbs and branches were left on the forest floor to decay. Unfortunately, the branches dried and all too often were prone to catch fire.

Forest fires were a constant hazard for the men working the woods. But the fires were also a source of concern for the ships on the lakes.

The burning trees produced huge amounts of smoke. The smoke often hung low over the water, making visibility worse than in fog causing many maritime accidents.

The smoke from the onshore blaze laid low on the water. Captain Ennes looked out the wheelhouse windows. He wished he could see land to verify his position, but the smoke obstructed his view of shore.

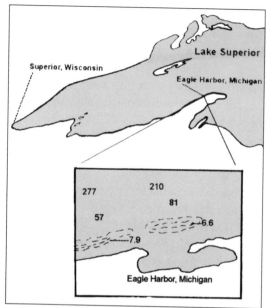

The William C. Moreland *struck Sawtooth Reef off Eagle Bay, Michigan. The numbers in the lower drawing indicate depths in feet.*

Two hundred miles into the trip, at about 9:00 PM, the 580-foot ship traveling at full speed, suddenly ground to a stop. The *William Moreland* was not the 1-1/2 to 2 miles off the peninsula as they thought. Rather they were less than a mile and the ship had run up on Sawtooth Reef off Eagle Harbor, Michigan.

The notorious Sawtooth Reef has seen the demise of many ships. The 254-foot steamer Colorado in 1898 and the 65-foot tug, Fern were lost on the reef in 1901 while trying to salvage the Colorado. The *Moreland* would not be the last to meet the reef either. In 1919 the 258-foot iron packet freighter *Tioga* was destroyed by the reef.

Captain Ennes ordered the telegraph to full astern in an attempt to back the ship off the reef. The three-month-old ship wasn't budging; it had run hard aground on the jagged rocky reef just a few feet below the surface.

The *Moreland* had sustained damage to her hull and began taking on water. The crew fought to slow the incoming torrents of water, but by morning a storm started blowing and Captain Ennes ordered the men to the waiting boats of the Portage Ship Canal Lifesaving station. The ship wasn't in jeopardy of sinking; she was hard aground.

Once the storm had blown out, the captain and crew were able to return to their ship. They raised steam in her boilers but before an attempt at powering off the reef could be made, it was found that the large steel ship had developed a crack between hatches 10 and 11. The brand new ship, supported on the reef at her bow, with an un-supported aft began to break in two.

Tom Reid, owner of Reid Wrecking and Towing Company, was awarded the bid to salvage the *William C. Moreland*. He and a crew set out from their quarters at Sarnia, Canada aboard the wrecking tugs *Manistique* and *Sarnia*.

Under the direction of the captain, almost 7,000 tons of iron ore were removed from the *Moreland* in hopes that the lighter craft might be able to be repaired and floated free of the reef. Unfortunately the big vessel was held fast to the rocky bottom.

Captain Reid continued to remove the cargo but they were often chased from the lake by the tremendous fall storms that lash out at Lake Superior. In a violent storm, the *Moreland* cracked between hatches 22 and 23. The once new 580-foot long ship was now divided into three pieces! Due to the storms and the onset of heavy ice, the salvaging of the wreck of the *William C. Moreland* had to be put off until spring.

When the weather cleared, the open ends of the broken vessel were closed in with temporary bulkheads and pumped out. Then in July of 1911 the three sections were lashed together and floated free of the reef.

While being towed, the *Moreland*, incapable of steering, collided with the tug James Reid. The temporary patches began to leak and the ship took on more water than the pumps could handle. The *William C. Moreland* once again sank on Sawtooth Reef. This time the vessel was on a deeper part of the reef and only part of her superstructure remained visible.

Another severe Lake Superior storm pounded down on the crippled vessel separating the 278-foot stern section from the other two sections. Efforts were turned to salvaging the valuable stern section with its new triple expansion steam engines. They could be recovered and sold for use in another ship.

The stern section of the William C. Moreland *being towed by a Reid tug. From the State of Michigan Archive. Lansing, Michigan.*

The only time "Half" of a boat locked through at the Soo. From the State of Michigan Archive. Lansing, Michigan.

The stern section was temporarily repaired, raised by mid August and the Reid Wrecking and Towing Company towed the stern of the once brand new *William C. Moreland* almost 550 miles to Detroit.

The bow sections of the *Moreland* in time were assaulted by other storms and eventually slid off the reef into deeper water. The stern section was moved again to Port Huron where she was beached, waiting for someone to place a bid on her scrap value.

The *William C. Moreland*, 580-feet in length 58-feet wide and only months old when she ran up hard on Sawtooth Reef now almost two years earlier, was not going to go easily to the scrap yard. Fortunately, the Canadian Steamship Lines saw some usefulness left in the wreck and purchased it.

Construction began on a new 322-foot bow section in Superior, Wisconsin. The Reid Wrecking and Towing Company again took the remains of the *William C. Moreland* stern back up to Lake Superior to mate with her new forward section.

The new, actually half new, ship was christened in November of 1916 the *Sir Trevor Dawson*. The vessel sailed on the lakes until World War One when she was laid up. In 1920 the *Dawson* was sold and became the *Charles L. Hutchinson*.

She continued to be a profitable carrier and in 1951 her name was again changed, this time to *Gene C. Hutchings*. In 1962 another sale brought about another name change to *Parkdale*.

The once mighty *William C. Moreland* was retired in 1968. Throughout those years, the vessel saw a lot of service on the lakes and tragedy as well. In June of 1970 the ship sailed her last voyage. The last trip was to Cartagena, Spain for an appointment at the scrap yard. But the ship had beaten the odds and survived to a ripe old age of fifty eight... well half of her anyway.

SHIPS AT LEAST 500 FEET
GEORGE M. HUMPHREY

The Straits of Mackinaw, separating the upper and lower peninsulas of Michigan is a crowded waterway. Ships passing to and from Lake Michigan to ports on the other Great Lakes must pass through this narrow 4 mile wide passage where the weather and currents can be treacherous.

The Straits are also one of the locations on the Great Lakes which is known all too well for its fog. There are many ships which met their demise in this area; the *Cedarville* when it collided with the *Topdalsfjord*, and the collision between the *S.S. Elton Hoyt II* and the *S.S. Enders M. Voorhees* just to name two.

On June 15, 1943 two other ships collided in a dense fog, heavily damaging one and sinking the other.

The American Ship Building Company of Lorain, Ohio built the *George M. Humphrey* for the Kinsman Transit Company in 1927. At a length of 586-feet in length and 60-feet in beam she could carry large loads making a fine profit for her owners.

At 2:50 AM on June 15, 1943 the *Humphrey* was on a westerly course through the Straits of Mackinaw after having taken on a load of 13,992 tons

George M. Humphrey   586 Feet in Length

The George M. Humphrey. *From the Hugh Clark Great Lakes Photography collection.*

of iron ore bound for South Chicago, Illinois. Also in the Straits that morning traveling east was the 600-foot Great Lakes steamer *D. M. Clemson* of the Pittsburg Steamship Company.

In 1943 there were no satellite global positioning systems to guide a ship through the dense fog and no radar to look for other ships. During times of low visibility a captain could only reduce his speed, sound a fog signal and post lookouts to listen for the fog signals of nearby ships.

Unfortunately, these precautions were not enough. The *D.M. Clemson* about two miles off the Old Mackinaw Point rammed the *George M. Humphrey*, almost broadside. The two ships, moving at slow speeds saw each other appear out of the fog, and neither could prevent the collision, but both were able to warn their crews of the impending impact. No one on the *D.M. Clemson* was killed or injured and there were no fatalities or injuries on the *Humphrey*.

The two ships separated and with the general alarm blaring, the crew of the *Humphrey* tried to use the collision tarpaulin to reduce the water pouring through the gash in its hull. The *Humphrey* was damaged both above and below the waterline and the tarpaulin and the pumps could not keep the water out. It was just a matter of time before the big ship would sink.

The master of the *George M. Humphrey* sounded the abandon ship alarm.

The *D.M. Clemson* was badly damaged but not in jeopardy of sinking and stood by the *Humphrey* to pick up survivors. Another ship, the *Lagonda*, anchored nearby waiting better weather, heard the frantic whistles and went to lend assistance. Thirty one crew of the *Humphrey* climbed aboard the *Lagonda* and eight others were rescued by the *D. M. Clemson* as the *Humphrey* settled to the bottom in 80-feet of water, less than 20 minutes after the collision.

The *D.M. Clemson* was able make port under her own power and was eventually repaired and had a long career on the Great Lakes, eventually being scrapped in 1986.

The *George M. Humphrey* was a different story. The ship was sunk in 80-feet of water with only her masts rising above the surface.

The Kinsman Transit Company surrendered the ship to the insurance underwriters and was paid the sum of $860,000. The underwriters turned the ship over the United States Corps of Engineers for removal.

The *Humphrey*, laying directly in the course used by the Mackinaw Straits ferries between Mackinaw City and St. Ignace, posed a navigational hazard. The Corps of Engineers advertised for a contractor who would remove the *Humphrey* or dynamite the sunken hulk to provide a depth over the wreck of 35-feet.

Most salvagers that looked at the contract were only interested in the fast and easy solution of blowing the deckhouses and masts off the ship to the required depth, but Captain John Roen had another idea.

Captain Roen of Sturgeon Bay, Wisconsin negotiated terms that would give him until October 1, 1944 to remove the *Humphrey* or demolish it to a proven clear passage over her hulk.

The D.M. Clemson. *From the collections of the Port Huron Museum.*

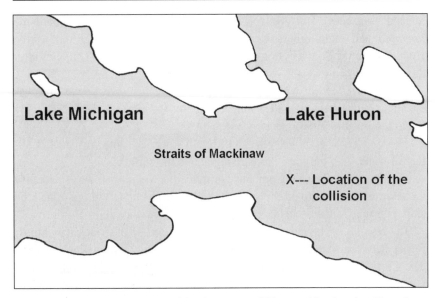

Captain Roen was a shrewd businessman. If he could raise the *Humphrey* he would be given the 586-foot ship. He could repair it and add to his own fleet. The estimated value of the *George M. Humphrey* at the time of the collision was one million dollars. But, if he could not raise the ship by the date he would have to demolish the hulk to the required clear depth at his own cost. Captain Roen was willing to take the gamble.

The steam ship Lagonda. *From the collections of the Port Huron Museum.*

The George M Humphrey *on the surface again! From the collection of the Door County Maritime Museum.*

When Captain Roen announced that he would attempt to raise the *Humphrey*, most people scoffed. The ship was 80-feet below the surface in an area where the currents could be treacherous, the weather was always a factor and the season was short. In those conditions how could he raise an almost

The tug Roen III *tows the* George M. Humphrey *to Sturgeon Bay, Wisconsin for refitting. From the collection of the Door County Maritime Museum.*

The Humphrey *sailing under the name of* Adam E. Cornelius. *From the Hugh Clark Great Lakes Photograph collection.*

600-foot long ship in less than one year? Captain Roen was out to prove the skeptics wrong.

In the late fall of 1943 Captain Roen began his salvage operation of the *Humphrey.* Two barges were anchored over the ship and the scoop bucket of a crane was lowered into the cargo hold to remove as much of the 13,992 tons of iron ore as possible. The removal and sale of the iron ore would lighten the ship and provide funds for the salvage operation.

The Humphrey *sailing as the Consumer Power. From the collections of the Port Huron Museum.*

When winter's ice closed off access to the wreck, Captain Roen was obsessed in planning the process of raising the *Humphrey*. He built a model of the ship and a water tank to work out the details of raising the ship.

Captain Roen's plan to raise the ship was relatively simple. He would partially submerge a barge, the *Maitland*, over the wreck then attach 50 cables from the barge to the *Humphrey* then pump air into the barge. The air would cause the barge to rise, lifting the steamer off the bottom about six feet. Tugs would then drag the *Humphrey* along the bottom until she again grounded.

The process would be repeated eight times until the *George M. Humphrey* was moved one and a half miles into shallower water. The ship was now so shallow the barge could not be used above the *Humphrey*, so the *Maitland* and another barge were positioned on either side of the partially submerged ship.

Lowering the two barges and filling them with air then raised the *Humphrey*. The foreword structure of the *Humphrey* was first to break the surface followed by the after structure and then the hatch covers as the ship continued to rise.

With the ship still partially submerged divers began to apply a temporary patch of timber over the hole in the *Humphrey's* starboard side. Once the patch was installed the water was pumped out of the ship and the *George M. Humphrey* floated free.

The *Humphrey* was towed from the Straits of Mackinaw across northern Lake Michigan to Sturgeon Bay, Wisconsin to be repaired and put back into service, and renamed the Captain John Roen in honor of her salvager.

Throughout its long career the ship held several names: the ship operated as the *George M. Humphrey* since her launch in 1927 until 1945, from 1945 until 1947 was named the Captain John Roen, sold in 1947 she became the Adam E. Cornelius and in 1957 she was again renamed Consumers Power.

The collision of the *George M. Humphrey* and the *D.M. Clemson* and the sinking of the *Humphrey* during a foggy night was tragic, but the raising of the sunken ship by the innovative Captain John Roen was a work of art.

SHIPS AT LEAST 500 FEET
DANIEL J. MORRELL

The Great lakes are well known for their fall storms. Cold Arctic air blows in from Canada and combines with the still relatively warm waters of the lakes and forms weather systems with ferocious winds and driving rain or blinding snow. Some of the weather systems that develop from the combination are typical fall storms but others become extremely violent. They are often called the "Witch of November", because they are the worst storms of the decade or sometimes the century. The Storm of November 29, 1966 was one of the wicked ones.

As the storm tracked south it dumped up to 15 inches of snow on Michigan's Upper Peninsula and the 70 mile per hour wind gusts created 7-foot snowdrifts paralyzing cities and towns and anything else in its path.

Hundreds of students from Michigan Technological University and Northern Michigan University returning from Thanksgiving break abandoned their snowbound cars to seek shelter.

Twenty to thirty foot waves and hurricane force winds raised havoc on all of the Great Lakes. The Chesapeake and Ohio ferry, City of Midland 41, while entering Ludington Harbor was blown onto a sandy reef.

Daniel J. Morrell   586 Feet in Length

A painting of the Daniel J. Morrell *by Marine Artist Robert McGreevy.*
Http://www.mcgreevy.com.

When he arrived at the Soo Locks, Captain Peter Pulcer master of the Columbia Transportation Company's *Edmund Fitzgerald*, reported that he had battled the storm all of the way across Lake Superior. Nine years later the *Edmund Fitzgerald* would run into another severe storm on Lake Superior and the ship and its crew would not fare as well.

Five days earlier the 470-foot West German Freighter *Nordmeer* abruptly grounded on a shoal near Alpena, Michigan. At the time the weather was clear with little wind and the shoal was clearly marked with a lighted buoy. But, through pilot error the ship ran hard aground on Thunder Bay Island Shoal.

Within minutes the cargo holds and the engine room began to fill from the breech in her hull. An S.O.S. was sent from the ship and the first to respond was the Canadian freighter Samuel Mather.

The Mather lowered a lifeboat and took thirty-five of the 43 sailors off the German Freighter. Remaining onboard were the captain and seven others to protect the salvage rights of the cargo and ship.

Nordmeer   470 Feet in Length

DANIEL J. MORRELL

The steamer Samuel Mather *passing through the St. Clair River at Port Huron. From the Hugh Clark Great Lakes Photograph Collection.*

On November 29, the day of the big storm, waves pounded the grounded *Nordmeer* relentlessly. Each wave forced the ship higher onto the rocky shoal, breaking the keel of the freighter and ripping out her bottom. The captain, fearing for the lives of his remaining crew, sent out an S.O.S. The eight men wanted off the violently rolling freighter. They had two motorized lifeboats at their disposal, but the conditions were too terrible to launch.

The Coast Guard Cutter Mackinaw left its homeport at once but it was still several hours away. A Coast Guard helicopter took off towards the grounded ship but winds hampered its attempts to rescue the crew. Fortunately, there was a slight lull in the storm and the helicopter took advantage of it to lift the men to safety.

The *Daniel J. Morrell* of the Bethlehem Fleet, was one of the large freighters that ventured out into Lake Huron on November 29, 1966.

The *Morrell* was launched in 1906 from the West Bay City Ship Building Company of Bay City, Michigan. At the time the 586-foot long *Morrell* was the largest ship ever to be built at the West Bay City yard.

The ship carried taconite pellets, coal and limestone in her three cargo holds that was loaded and un-loaded through 18 twelve by thirty six foot hatches. Since the *Morrell* was not equipped with a self un-loader she was unloaded by clamshell buckets lowered into her cargo holds.

The sides of the cargo holds were often damaged by the bucket hitting the sides of the hold allowing some leaking from the ballast tanks into the holds. The leaks were not considered a problem.

When the *Daniel J. Morrell* arrived at the Bethlehem Steel Plant at Buffalo, New York to off load its cargo the crew thought it was their last trip of the season, but the company told them that due to contractual agreements and mechanical problems with another ship that they had to make one more trip. It would be their 34th trip of the 1966 season.

While the ship was being un-loaded, two of the *Morrell* crew, John Groh of Erie, Pennsylvania and Dennis Hale of Ashtabula, Ohio, took the opportunity to visit their families. But, the un-loading took less time than they anticipated and when they arrived back at Buffalo they saw the *Morrell* steaming out of the harbor.

They made a radio call to the ship and were told to meet the *Morrell* at the Consolidated Fuel Dock in Windsor, Ontario when the ship stopped to take on 221 tons of stoker coal. The two sailors almost missed the last trip of the season... the last trip of the *Daniel J. Morrell.*

Due to storms on the lakes Captain Crawley anchored below Detroit to wait for better weather. After taking on coal the ship made its way through Lake St. Clair into the St. Clair River where Captain Crawley again anchored waiting for the conditions on Lake Huron to improve.

The sister ship of the *Morrell*, the *Edward Y. Townsend*, had departed Buffalo about the time the *Morrell* had. Like its sister the *Townsend* was making one last trip to Taconite, Minnesota.

Captain Crawley, of the *Morrell*, and master of the *Townsend*, Captain Connelly, remained in radio communication, discussing the storm and conditions in Lake Huron.

They also communicated with down-bound ships about the weather on Lake Huron. The report was light westerly winds 6-18 miles per hour, with building seas, nothing the *Townsend* or *Morrell* hadn't faced in their 60 year

The Daniel J. Morrell. *From the State of Michigan Archives, Lansing, Michigan.*

careers. On November 28, 1966 the two ships departed the St. Clair River and steamed into Lake Huron.

Sixty miles up into Lake Huron, at about 8:30 PM, the *Edward Y. Townsend* radioed the *Morrell*. The captains discussed the weather. The winds were from the north at 35 miles per hour and gusting with the waves running eight feet.

An hour and a half later the two captains again conferred about the weather. The winds had increased to fifty miles per hour out of the north and the waves were over twelve feet.

Captain Connelly reported that his ship was pounding on the seas and rolling. He restricted crew from being on the open deck. On the *Morrell*, several miles ahead of the *Townsend*, Captain Crawley said the winds and seas were so bad they were steering 347 degrees just to hold a 341 degree course.

By 11:15 PM the conditions were rapidly deteriorating. The winds were 50 to 55 miles per hour and the waves still building.

The captains discussed turning around and heading back to the St. Clair River. But, Captain Connelly considered it safer to head into the sea rather than turn and take the waves on the stern. He was also concerned that since they did not have cargo they might not be heavy enough to come about in the waves and not be able to get out of the trough of the waves. Another option the two captains discussed was to anchor in the protected waters of Thunder Bay.

At ten minutes to midnight Captain Crawly called the *Townsend* but was told by Captain Connelly, "I will call you back," and hung up.

The *Townsend* had begun to blow around, or broach into the sea. The ship fell off to starboard and left full rudder was required before the ship was brought back on course and out of the trough of the waves. When Captain Connelly later reported the incident to Captain Crawley, Crawley said they had had a similar situation but all was well.

The wind had increased to 65 miles per hour and the seas, which Captain Connelly described as "tremendous", were running at 20- to 25-feet. The *Townsend* reported she was pitching, rolling and pounding in the seas and several times solid water was taken over the bow.

The *Morrell* and *Townsend* were not the only ships out on Lake Huron when the weather took a turn for the worse. The 451-foot freighter *Howard L. Shaw* was heading north on Lake Huron barely able to make one mile per hour through the wind and waves. The helmsman struggled at the wheel to keep the ship's bow into the wind. He had to swing the wheel fully from port to starboard trying to maintain control when a tremendous gust blew the *Shaw* around until it was heading south!

The *Howard L. Shaw* tried twice to come about and regain its northern course, but both attempts failed so they continued on south seeking shelter at Sarnia, Ontario.

The captain of the *S.S. Fred A. Manske* reported his ship was almost blown around but they were able to fight it. He said he was reluctant to come about in the seas because the self un-loading equipment made the *Manske* top heavy and he was afraid it would roll in the seas. The ship made it past the dangerous Point Aux Barques area and arrived safely at its destination.

The 615-foot *S.S. Harry Coulby* was about six miles north of Port Sanilac, Michigan reported it took solid water over her bow from a huge wave. The captain was informed via radio that conditions further north were much worse. He gave the orders to come about and set a course back to Port Huron.

The 586-foot *S.S. Robert Hobson* was 4 miles north of the Harbor Beach light when it too it was blown around and elected not to attempt to come about in the heavy seas and continued south to the St. Clair River.

When the 592-foot *S.S. Kinsman Independent*, loaded with coal, passed through the St. Clair River into southern Lake Huron the Captain Newman reported that the winds were light and from the west. Sixty miles north while off the Harbor Beach Light the conditions had changed. The winds were coming from the north at 50 to 60 miles per hour. The *Kinsman Independent* was blown off course and wallowed in the trough of the waves for a few fearful minutes before it was able to get out of the trough and head back to the safety of Port Huron.

The Fred A. Manske *in calmer waters. From the Hugh Clark Great Lakes Photograph Collection.*

On the *Townsend* and *Morrell* the engineers were kept busy during the trip up Lake Huron. The storm prevented the ships from running at full speed but the huge waves and ferocious wind continually tried to push the bow of the ships to starboard. At times the bridge called for full speed for the power to keep the bow into the wind. But, when the stern was lifted out of the water by the waves the engineers had to reduce the RPM's of the propeller. A propeller turning at full speed without the resistance of the water would turn too fast and do serious damage to the propulsion machinery. The engineers had to reduce speed every two minutes when the ships were running at full.

Captain Connelly of the *Townsend* later stated that the weather and sea conditions off Point Aux Barques, towards the top of Michigan's "Thumb" was far worse than the predicted expected conditions. He said he could not recall having experienced sea conditions of this magnitude on the Great Lakes.

Dennis Hale, the watchman who missed the *Morrell's* departure at Buffalo stood watch in the pilothouse from 4:00 PM until he was relieved at 8:00 PM. At that time it was snowing and blowing some but the weather was not severe enough to prevent him from walking the length of the exposed spar deck to the stern for dinner and back forward when he was done.

Watchman Hale went to his room on the forward starboard side spar deck. As the storm intensified he could hear the anchors beat against the ship as the *Morrell* pounded in the seas.

Hale slept until 2:00 AM when he was awaken by a loud "Bang." Followed a few minutes later by another loud "Bang" and the sound of books falling from his bookshelf. He reached for his bunk light and found it didn't work, then the general alarm sounded.

Clothed only in his under shorts and life preserver, Hale left his room and went to the starboard passageway. There were not any lights on in the forward section of the ship but looking aft he saw the stern was still lit. He also saw the middle of the ship was higher than the stern section, the *Daniel J. Morrell* was "hogging." The ship was in the process of breaking at the center.

Dennis Hale ran back to his room looking for clothes but in the dark could only find his pea coat. He grabbed it and ran to the forward life raft. He stood with other members of the forward deck crew.

They climbed into the raft and held on tight waiting for the ship to slip below the waves and the raft to float free. The men on the raft included the captain, first and second mate, Hale and others who worked in the forward deckhouse. They sat in the raft and watched a visual and audio nightmare unfold before them. The stern portion tore away from the bow section near hatches 11 and 12 with steam shooting out of broken pipes at the point of separation. The stern, still under power, repeatedly smashed into the bow section until the bow was forced to port at about a 90-degree angle to the stern. The sounds of metal grinding against metal, steel plates being ripped, rivets snapped and the roar of the storm and crash of waves completed the horrible scenario.

What seemed to take an eternity was only eight minutes between the sounding of the general alarm and when the bow began to settle and the life raft was washed off the starboard side.

The men waiting at the forward life raft were thrown into the cold November Lake Huron water.

Dennis Hale rose to the surface gasping for air. He saw the empty raft several feet away and swam towards it. By the time he got to it there John Cleary and Art Stojek had climbed onboard.

The men helped Hale climb onto the raft and a few minutes later they found Charles Fosbender in the water and helped him onto the raft. The four

The front page of the Thursday, December 1, 1966, Bay City Times *cries out the news of the Great Lakes freighter* Daniel J. Morrell *had broke and sunk in Lake Huron. The top headline is a Father Cornelius McEachin's answer to sole survivor Dennis Hales' hunting question: "Father, why am I alive?"*

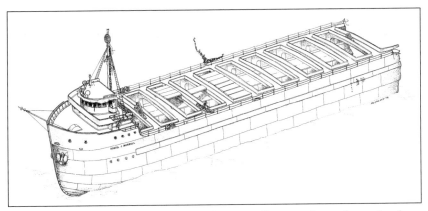

This drawing by Marine Artist Robert McGreevy shows how the bow section of the Daniel J. Morrell *lies on the bottom of Lake Huron. Http://www.mcgreevy.com.*

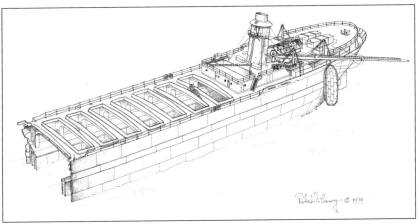

The stern section of the Morrell *based on information available in 1979. Since then it was found the ship broke between hatched 8 and 9, and the lifeboat hanging off the port side has fallen to the bottom. By Marine Artist Robert McGreevy, http://www.mcgreevy.com.*

men looked for others but never found anyone else. The men held on while the raft rose high on the huge waves then fell low into the trough in the pitch black night.

When the raft crested on the waves the men could see through the snow a very disturbing site; the stern of the *Morrell*, lights still burning, steaming away from them and the bow pointing towards the sky as it slipped beneath the waves.

In the storage compartment on the raft the men found a flare gun, hand held flares, a sea anchor, a can of oil for the anchor and a flashlight.

With freezing fingers the men fired off the flares but there were not any ships close enough to see them.

The hurricane force winds blew the snow and cold lake water spray, stinging the men's exposed skin. The shivering men, soaking wet, could only lay down, pray and hang on to the raft as it was tossed around by the waves.

The storm continued to lash the lake through the night. At dawn John Cleary and Art Stojek were unresponsive, they had passed on during the night. Dennis Hale called Fosbender who weakly answered.

Charlie Fosbender hung on till 4:00 PM, fourteen hours after the *Morrell* had broken in two, when he succumbed to the storm and cold.

The *Edward Y. Townsend* battled its way through the storm and arrived at Sault Ste. Marie. Captain Connelly questioned when the *Daniel J. Morrell* had locked through and was told that the *Morrell* had not yet arrived. Captain Connelly promptly notified the Bethlehem Steel headquarters in Cleveland, Ohio that the *Morrell* was overdue. Amazingly, the company waited almost a full day before informing the Coast Guard of the missing *Daniel J. Morrell*.

Once told of the missing steamer, the Coast Guard sent out a notice to all mariners that the *Daniel J. Morrell* was overdue and asked all ships to keep an eye out for her. Sailing through a storm as vicious as this one, anything could have happened. A ship could have lost all of its electronics, including the radio, the ship could be otherwise disabled and sheltering in some desolate cove.

The mystery of the *Morrell* began to unravel when the G.G. Post recovered the body of a sailor in a lifejacket with the name *Morrell* stenciled on it. An empty life raft, life ring and several more bodies from the *Morrell* were found and everyone knew the *Daniel J. Morrell* must have met with disaster during the storm that ravaged the Great Lakes that November day in 1966.

It wasn't until 38 hours after the ship had sunk that the story surrounding the sinking of the *Daniel J. Morrell* came to light. That is when the forward life raft with 4 men was found along the Michigan shore. Onboard the raft were Art Stojek, John Cleary, Charles Fosbender and Dennis Hale. All had succumbed to the elements except Dennis Hale.

Watchman Hale, from his bed at Harbor Beach Hospital, suffering terribly from exposure, told of the demise of the freighter *Daniel J. Morrell*.

The 586-foot long *Daniel J. Morrell* was broken in two by the storm! The bow quickly sank and the stern powered some 5 miles away before it sank.

Captain Connelly, master of the *Townsend*, conducted a heavy weather damage survey of his ship. He was concerned for his ship after battling through the tremendous storm that assaulted Lake Huron and had broken and sunk the *Daniel J. Morrell*. A crack one eighth inch wide by eighteen inch long was found on the deck extending from the combing of the hatch cover towards the center of the ship.

Almost immediately, the Marine Inspection Bureau pulled the sailing certificate of the *Edward Y. Townsend*. They deemed the ship un-seaworthy. Without a certificate, the ship could not be used to carry cargo or crew. The *Townsend* was never repaired.

On a cold and stormy November day in 1966 the "Witch of November" struck Lake Huron. The huge *Daniel J. Morrell* that had sailed the lakes for 60 years was ripped apart and sent to the bottom. She was on her last trip of the season, a trip she wasn't even scheduled to make, but fate sent the *Daniel J. Morrell* out on Lake Huron on that November night. Unfortunately, it was also fate that took twenty eight men to their deaths, only Dennis Hale miraculously lived through the ordeal.

In Honor of the Crew of the *Daniel J. Morrell*

Listed as Dead or Missing

Arthur I. Crawley,	Master	47	Rocky River, OH
Phillip E. Kapets	1st Mate	51	Ironwood, MI
Duncan R. MacLeod	2nd Mate	61	Gloucester, MA
Ernest G. Marcotte	3rd Mate	62	Pontiac, MI
Charles H Fosbender	Wheelsman	42	St. Clair, MI
Henry Rischmiller	Wheelsman	34	Williamsville, NY
Stuart A. Campbell	Wheelsman	60	Marinette, WI
Albert P. Whoeme	Watchman	51	Knife River, MN
Norman M. Bragg	Watchman	40	Niagara Falls NY
Larry G. Davis	Deckwatch	27	Toledo, OH
John M. Groh	Deckwatch	21	Erie, PA
Arthur E. Stojek	Deckhand	41	Buffalo, NY
John J. Cleary, Jr.	Deckhand	20	Cleveland, OH
John H. Schmidt	Chief Engineer	46	Toledo, OH
Valmour Marchildon	1st Asst. Eng.	43	Kenmore, NY
Alfred G. Norkunas	2nd Asst. Eng.	39	Superior, WI
George A Dahl	3rd Asst. Eng.	38	Duluth, MN
Wilson E. Simpson	Oiler	50	Albemarle, NC

Donald E. Worcester	Oiler	38	Columbia Falls,,ME
Arthur S. Fargo	Fireman	52	Ashtabula, OH
Chester Konieczka	Fireman	45	Hamburg, NY
Saverio Grippi	Coalpasser	53	Ashtabula, OH
Leon R, Truman	Coalpasser	45	Toledo, OH
David L. Price	Coalpasser	19	Cleveland, OH
Nicholas Homick	2nd Cook	35	Hudson, PA
Stanley J. Satlawa	Steward	39	Buffalo, NY
Joseph A. Mahsem	Porter	59	Duluth, MN
Charles Sestakauskas	Porter	49	Buffalo, NY

Survivor

Dennis N. Hale	Watchman	26	Ashtabula, OH

SHIPS AT LEAST 500 FEET
CEDARVILLE

On November 17, 1958 a vicious Lake Michigan storm took the Bradley Transportation Line's freighter *Carl D. Bradley* and most of its crew to the bottom of Lake Michigan. The *Bradley's* homeport of Rogers City, Michigan was stunned. Of the 35 men of the crew of the *Bradley*, 32 called northern Michigan home, most from Rogers City.

The loss to the small northeast Michigan town was devastating. There wasn't a family that wasn't touched by the sinking. The men who died that stormy November night were husbands, fathers, sons and friends of those left behind.

On May 7, 1965, the *Alpena News* ran a headline which brought back memories of the *Bradley* sinking and also brought a new group of widows and fatherless children to Rogers City.

The *Cedarville* was a 588-foot self un-loading freighter owned by the U.S. Steel Corporation of New York and operated by the Bradley Transportation Line of Rogers City. Launched in 1927 as the A. F. Harvey , the ship underwent a conversion to a self un-loader in 1957 and her name was changed to *Cedarville*.

During her 38 year career, the *Cedarville* was a familiar sight on the Great Lakes. She primarily delivered limestone from the quarry at Calcite,

Cedarville   588 Feet in Length

The Cedarville *by Marine Artist Robert McGreevy.*
Http://www.mcgreevy.com.

Michigan (Near Rogers City in Michigan's Lower Peninsula) and Port Dolomite, Michigan (Near Cedarville, located on Michigan's Upper Peninsula) to steel mills on Lakes Erie and Michigan and the Detroit River.

Aboard the *Cedarville* on her last trip was a crew of 35 with Captain Martin Joppich as master. Captain Joppich was no stranger to the Great Lakes. In his 19 year career he had sailed through whatever the Great Lakes threw at him.

The Carl D. Bradley. *From the Bayliss Public Library, Sault Ste. Marie, Michigan.*

144

THE ALPENA NEWS

Spirit of '76
High Reflector 76 to M...
Scattered showers likely tonight

66th Year • No. 238 ... ...GAT, ... 12 PAG-2 3 CENTS

CEDARVILLE RAMMED, SINKS

Two Dead,
10 Missing,
23 Rescued

In the spring of 1965 the lake freighters were coming out from winter lay-up and steel mills were waiting for the ships to replenish their inventory of raw materials used in the production of steel. The economy was flourishing and the demand was great.

On May 7, 1965 the *Cedarville* took on 14,411 tons of open-hearth limestone at Calcite, Michigan to be delivered to the vast industrial complex at Gary, Indiana, a 300 mile trip the ship had made many times in her past.

The *Cedarville* departed Calcite at 5:00 AM and entered Lake Huron in a light fog. The ship set a heading for the Straights of Mackinaw and Captain Joppich called for full speed, about 12 miles per hour.

On the bridge the duty officers were the captain, Chief Officer Piechan, and Third Officer Cook. They closely monitored the radar, watching for other vessels, the radio direction finder, to determine their position and the gyro compass and Lake Survey charts No. 60 (Lake Huron-Straights of Mackinaw) and chart No. 6 (Straights of Mackinaw) were spread out on the chart table.

Completing the bridge crew that morning were Leonard Gabrysiak, at the helm and Ivan Trafelet who was standing watch on the port wing.

The ship followed the up-bound course making the necessary course changes as indicated on the chart.

When the *Cedarville* was off the Cheboygan traffic buoy, the captain reported that the fog had become denser and that visibility was less than a half mile.

There are many areas on the Great Lakes which, due to predominate weather patterns and unique geographical features, make them more prone for fog development. One area where fog as thick as the proverbial "Pea Soup" can be found is the Straights of Mackinaw.

The Straights of Mackinaw is a narrow passage that separates Michigan's Upper and Lower Peninsulas, and also where Lakes Michigan and Huron meet.

Captains on other ships in the Straights that day and police officers on shore reported visibility was drastically reduced by fog. Sometimes the

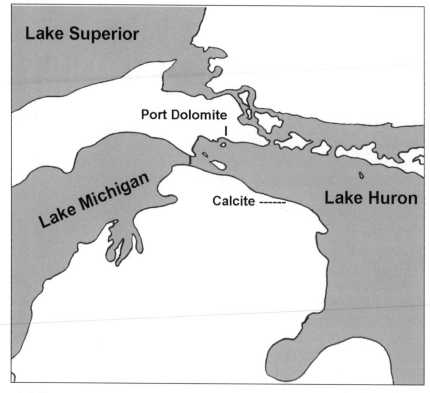

Lake Superior

Port Dolomite

Lake Michigan

Calcite ------

Lake Huron

visibility was in excess of a mile then there were thick patches where you couldn't see more than 50-feet.

On that May morning, there were other ships shrouded in the thick fog in the vicinity of the Mackinaw Straights.

The *Cedarville* saw on the radar a ship ahead of its position and established radio contact with the steamer *Benson Ford* which was heading east from the Mackinaw Bridge.

The two ships exchanged passing information, agreeing on a one whistle, or port-to-port passing. The two ships passed within a half of a mile without incident, although neither visually saw the other because of the thick layer of fog.

Captain Joppich had a radio conversation with another down-bound vessel, the German freighter *Weissenburg*. The *Weissenburg* requested a port-to-port passing and the *Cedarville* altered course slightly to give plenty of room for the passing.

The captain of the *Weissenburg* informed the *Cedarville* by radiotelephone that there was another ship in the area. The Norwegian ship *Topdalsfjord* was in fact ahead of the *Weissenburg* and heading east in the Mackinaw Straights.

The Cedarville *passing through the St. Clair River. From the Great Lakes Photograph collection of Hugh Clark.*

Captain Joppich attempted to reach the Norwegian ship to establish a passing agreement. There was no response.

The lookout, Ivan Trafelet, on the port wing of the bridge, reported to the captain hearing a fog signal coming from the approximate location of the Mackinaw Bridge.

The *Cedarville* was steaming through the fog at full speed, but when the report of the *Topdalsfjord* being in the area was heard, Captain Joppich ordered half-speed and a course change to the right.

The third mate, monitoring the radar screen, informed the captain that the ship was closing in on the *Cedarville*.

The 423-foot *Topdalsfjord* had taken on cargo in Milwaukee consigned for Fort William, Ontario on Lake Superior, a voyage which would take it through the Straights of Mackinaw.

Earlier in the day, Captain Haaland, master of the *Topdalsfjord*, was running at full speed but reduced to half when the visibility deteriorated. As the fog worsened and with reports of a

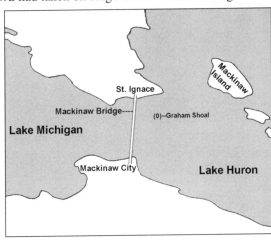

The United States Coast Guard Cutter Sundew. *From the collection of the Coast Guard Historians office.*

westbound ship approaching, the *Topdalsfjord's* speed was placed at dead slow ahead, only making 3-4 knots.

The lookouts on both ships looked into the deep fog and listened to the fog signals blasting the normally quiet morning hour.

"Ship!" Ivan Trafelet, on the *Cedarville* shouted as the bow of the *Topdalsfjord* appeared out of the fog only one hundred feet off the *Cedarville's* port bow.

Captain Joppich ordered the *Cedarville's* engine to full ahead in an attempt to pass in front of the bow of the *Topdalsfjord*. Once the bow was past, the captain ordered the wheel to port in hopes of swinging the ship's stern out of the path of the approaching ship.

The *Topdalsfjord* was approaching very slowly on a course that took it almost perpendicular to the *Cedarville*.

Captain Haaland ordered the engines on emergency full astern to quickly slow his ship and to avoid the *Cedarville*.

The crews of both ships stood silently watching and praying the evasive measures were enough, hoping the *Cedarville* would slide by in front of the *Topdalsfjord* being slowed by its reversing engine.

The bow of the *Cedarville* passed in front of the *Topdalsfjord* and the long gray hull of the *Cedarville* floated by, but not fast enough. The bow of the *Topdalsfjord* smashed into the port side of the *Cedarville* ripping the freighter open above and below the waterline.

The forward motion of the *Cedarville* pushed the *Topdalsfjord* aside and the two ships drifted apart.

The first eleven feet of the bow of the *Topdalsfjord* was severely damaged but the collision bulkhead had not been breached and water only flooded the fore peak.

Once he made sure his ship was not in danger of sinking, Captain Haaland ordered two boats from the *Topdalsfjord* to be lowered to search for any survivors from the *Cedarville*.

Following the collision, the *Cedarville's* engines were stopped, the general alarm was sounded, the port anchor dropped and a Mayday call was sent out. The crew immediately went about trying to cover the gash in the hull with an emergency tarpaulin, but the size of the hole was too large. Cold Lake Huron water poured into the No. 2 cargo hold. The ship immediately took on a list to starboard as lake water gushed in.

Any of the crew not working in the engine room or on the bridge, were ordered to lower the after port and starboard lifeboats to the spar deck and stood by awaiting further instructions. In addition to the lifeboats the ship had two life rafts designed to float free when the ship sinks.

Noting that the ship was taking on water but not in danger of immediately sinking, Captain Joppich ordered the anchor to be raised and the *Cedarville* to steam towards shore at full speed. The captain wanted to beach the ship in shallow water to save his crew and his ship.

Several more Mayday calls were made and the captain radioed other ships in the area warning them of his intentions and to stay out of his way. The *Weissenburg* upon hearing this changed her course to follow the *Cedarville* in her mad dash to safety.

A painting of the Cedarville *on the bottom by Marine Artist Robert McGreevy. Http://www.mcgreevy.*

The ship was sinking deeper from the water pouring through the gash in her hull as she covered 2.3 miles trying to make the shallow water by Mackinaw City. But, two miles from the beach the ship suddenly rolled over to starboard and sank.

The crew attempted to release the number 1 lifeboat as the ship rolled but were not successful and it was taken to the bottom with the ship. The number 2 lifeboat, with some crew, was released and floated free as the ship sank from under her. Both life rafts floated free, but most crew of the *Cedarville* did not have a chance to get into the lifeboat or rafts and were thrown into the frigid lake as the ship sank in 102-feet of water.

The lookouts on the *Weissenburg* heard the

The pilothouse of the Cedarville *as she lies on her starboard side on the bottom. From the collection of Kerry Whipple.*

screams from men in the water ahead of the ship and her lifeboats were immediately lowered to render assistance. Six survivors were pulled from the water and 21 others from the lifeboat and life raft were taken onboard the *Weissenburg.*

Coast Guard vessels from the Mackinaw Island station raced to the site and searched through the fog but did not find any more survivors. The search efforts were also assisted by an air unit of the Coast Guard and by the USCG ice breaker Mackinaw, and Coast Guard Cutters Naugatuck and Sundew.

There were many questions regarding Captain Joppich's judgment during and after the collision. Why did he attempt to beach the *Cedarville* at Mackinaw City, over 4 miles from the point of the collision when Graham Shoal was only one mile away and Old Mackinaw Point 2.2 miles.

The results of the collision of the Bradley Transportation Line's freighter *Cedarville* and the Motor Vessel *Topdalsfjord* were, $30,000 in damage to the Norwegian ship, loss of the *Cedarville* valued at $3,500,000, and loss of $21,000 in cargo.

A more important result of the collision were the 7 men who died, the 3 who were missing and presumed dead, and 16 injured.

Of the ten missing or dead, nine lived in Rogers City. The city again mourned.

Today the *Cedarville* is a popular site for recreational divers. The wreck lies on her starboard side in 105-feet of water. When diving the *Cedarville* much caution must be taken due to the depth, the swift Straits of Mackinaw current, the amount of debris scattered over the wreck and it is easy for a diver to become disoriented in the almost up-side-down wreck.

SHIPS AT LEAST 600 FEET
DONNACONA

"FIRE!"

A fire onboard a ship in open water is a sailor's worst nightmare.

There is nowhere to go. The crew must take a stand and fight the fire until it's out or until they have to abandon ship. Then they might have to fight to survive in open water in a small boat.

The Canadian Steamship Lines freighter *Donnacona* suffered a fire in the open water on December 16, 1964.

The 604-foot long *Donnacona* was launched from the Western Shipbuilding & Drydock Company at Port Arthur, Ontario in 1914 and originally named *Grant W. Morden*. From the time of her launch the ship reigned until 1926 as the longest ship on the lakes.

By 1964 she was still considered a large ship and had changed ownership and names; she was now the *Donnacona*.

On a mid December day of 1964 the ship was down-bound from the Canadian ports of Fort William and Port Arthur, Ontario on the western end of Lake Superior with a cargo of 400,000 bushels of grain bound for the Hiram Walker Distillery at Windsor, Ontario along the Detroit River.

Donnacona   604 Feet in Length

The 604-foot Donnacona *which caught fire in Lake Huron. From the Al Hart Collection.*

The crew of thirty men and two women were anxious to finish this trip; it was the last of the season. They would soon be home with their families.

The passage across Lake Superior, through the locks at Sault Ste. Marie and down into Lake Huron went as well as could be expected for mid December on the Great Lakes. The temperature was cold and a coating of ice formed on the ship's bow as the wind whipped waves broke on the ship.

Thirty miles north of Port Huron, where Lake Huron empties into the St. Clair River disaster struck.

About 10:00 AM, the third mate and the helmsman were on watch in the wheelhouse. When he first noticed the fire, the third mate hit the alarm button to the captain's quarters and reached for the radiotelephone to make a distress call. The radiotelephone was not working.

The alarm bell went off in Captain Harold Miller's cabin, a signal that he was needed on the bridge. The captain's cabin was in the foreword deckhouse below the wheelhouse. He opened his cabin door and quickly slammed it shut. The hall was filled with flames.

Captain Miller went to another door where he could climb an outside ladder to the wheelhouse but the wind blown flames prevented that path. He had no choice but to go down to the spar deck.

With no way to send a distress call, the third mate repeatedly sounded short whistle blasts in hopes that someone along the shore would notice the ship on fire and call authorities.

The Grant W. Morden *was the longest ship on the lakes from 1914 until 1926. From the Bayliss Public Library, Sault Ste. Marie, Michigan.*

There were 14 of the crew that bunked in cabins in the foreword section of the ship. Captain Miller made sure that they and the rest of the 32 crewmembers were on deck and accounted for. Captain Miller then directed most of the crew to begin fighting the fire with all the available onboard equipment while others prepared the lifeboats for launch in case it was necessary to abandon ship.

The crew needed to extinguish the fire but they also had to keep the flames from spreading to the highly flammable cargo of grain.

At 11:00 AM, an Air Force F-106 fighter jet was flying over Lake Huron on practice maneuvers when the pilot reported smoke bellowing from a ship in lower Lake Huron.

About the same time, the 415-foot *Wyandotte* coming

The Donnacona *after the fire ravaged the ship's pilothouse. From the Hartson Collection of the Port Huron Museum.*

down the lake noticed flames and dense smoke coming from the a ship south of her position and made a call to the Harbor Beach Coast Guard. The *Wyandotte* then steamed at full speed to assist the men and women aboard the burning *Donnacona*. The *Donnacona* crew was excited at the site of another ship racing towards them.

The *Wyandotte* tried to get along side the *Donnacona* but the winds and waves prevented it. She stood by in case the crew needed to abandon ship and relayed messages with their radio from the burning ship

The Coast Guard responded in full force. A boat from the Harbor Beach station raced the 30 miles to the scene while an amphibious airplane and a helicopter from the Air-Sea Rescue Unit stationed at Selfridge Air Base were dispatched.

At the foot of Lake Huron, the Lightship Huron lies at anchor guiding ships to the channel leading to the St. Clair River. On that December day the Coast Guard cutter *Acacia* was refueling the lightship. Upon hearing the distress call, the *Acacia* terminated the refueling and set course for the *Donnacona*.

The fire originated in a shaft below the pilothouse where electrical cables and hoses for the hydraulic steering pass. The shaft that extends from the keel

The US Coast vessel Guard Acacia. *From the collections of the United States Coast Guard Historical Office.*

up to the wheelhouse acted as a funnel for the flames to reach all the way up through the foreword deckhouse.

Captain Miller spoke of the speed of the fire; "Everything went at once. It didn't start somewhere and creep somewhere else. It was everywhere at once."

The fire in the shaft destroyed all means to communicate, operate the engines and steer the boat. The *Donnacona* was adrift in the lake. The wind and waves pushed the ship further out into the lake as the crew fought to gain control of the fire ravaging their ship. By time the USCG cutter *Acacia* arrived on site, the *Donnacona* had been blown six miles from the point the fire was first discovered.

After a valiant three hour firefight, the crew had brought the fire under control and the *Donnacona* wallowed in the lake, lifelessly, still smoldering. The pilothouse, captain's and mates, cabins were totally destroyed, the foreword crew cabins suffered both smoke and water damage. But, the entire crew was safe.

The USCG cutter *Acacia* took the stricken ship in tow and pulled her to Port Huron where two Great Lakes Towing tugs, the Superior and Maine took the *Donnacona* down to Windsor to discharge her cargo.

SHIPS AT LEAST 600 FEET
FRONTENAC

Ships can get into trouble in any number of ways. They sometimes collide into each other during periods of low visibility due to fog or snow. Some ships break apart in storms or develop a leak and sink. There are ships that sail away from the dock never to be seen again and then there are vessels lost or damaged due to human error, and sometimes ships just run aground.

The 604-foot long *Frontenac* was one that ran aground.

The Great Lakes freighter *Frontenac* of the Cleveland-Cliffs fleet was launched at River Rouge, Michigan in 1927. At 604-feet the *Frontenac* was one of the larger ships on the lakes. Throughout her career, the ship carried millions of tons of iron ore from the company's mines in Minnesota and Michigan down the Great Lakes to the steel mills located on lower Lake Michigan, Lake Erie and along the Detroit River.

In late July of 1958, the *Frontenac* had steamed into Buffalo, New York with a cargo of iron ore. The trip down had been uneventful like the many others the ship had made that season. They discharged their cargo and prepared to take on a load of coal bound for a northern port, then take on iron ore for the return trip.

Frontenac   604 Feet in Length

The Frontenac. *From the collections of the Port Huron Museum.*

Lines were cast off and two tugs slowly pulled the big ship from the dock. The *Frontenac* was turned around and she blew a whistle of thanks to the tugs as her propellers churned up the muddy water of the Buffalo River.

As the ship steamed out of the river building speed, she began to make the curve towards the main entrance of the harbor and the open water of Lake Erie.

A Coast Guardsman assigned to the Buffalo Breakwall Lighthouse watched the *Frontenac* departing and realized the ship seemed to be swinging a bit wider that necessary. He watched until he realized that if the ship did not alter its course it might run into the breakwall.

The Guardsman called his watch-mate and the two men yelled, waved their arms and jumped up and down trying to catch the attention of the ship.

When someone on the bridge did notice their present course would result in a collision, they attempted to slow the ship and alter its course. The *Frontenac* was put into full astern, the wheel put hard to starboard and the rumble of chain could be heard as an anchor was dropped.

Any measures taken were in vain as the 604-foot *Frontenac* rammed bow on into the foundation crib supporting the lighthouse.

The lighthouse, built in 1872 was a two and a half story brick building, approximately 24-feet square, with the light tower rising several feet higher. The massive foundation crib built of large square cut timber, covered with concrete, and filled with large stones was sunk to the lake's bottom.

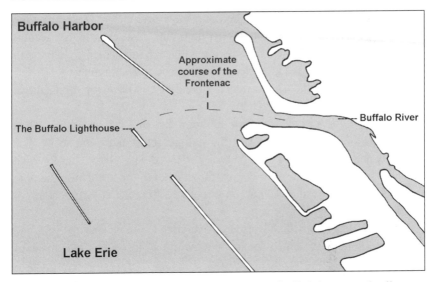

The impact of the *Frontenac* was so great that the lighthouse and crib were pushed back twenty feet and the lighthouse building was leaning at a 15 degree angle.

The *Frontenac* sustained damage to her bow but its collision bulkhead had not been breeched. The ship sailed under her own power to a Buffalo dock to begin repairs.

The Buffalo Breakwall lighthouse light was extinguished until a temporary light was installed. The citizens of Buffalo affectionately called the lighthouse the "Leaning tower of Buffalo".

In 1961 the damaged lighthouse was removed and a new light structure was built in its place.

Eleven years later the *Frontenac* again met with disaster.

In late November of 1979, the *Frontenac* was steaming across Lake Superior. The 604-foot ship was bound for Silver Bay, Minnesota to take on a load of iron ore destined for a lower lake steel mill.

The weather on the lake that late November day was typical of the time of year; snow, gusty winds and high seas.

The *Frontenac*, piloted by Captain Clyde P. Trueax, searched the harbor looking for the lighted beacon on Pellet Island that he should see south of his position. He needed the light to determine his position. The ship, moving a bare steerage speed, slowly nosed her way into the Silver Bay harbor entrance.

What the captain did not know was that the light had been extinguished by the storm and the *Frontenac* had been blown off course. The ship was actually south of the entrance channel.

The huge ship was operating blind in a snow squall. The winds from the north were blowing at over 30 miles per hour with gusts even higher accompanied by wind whipped waves, growing with each moment. The helmsman held the wheel tightly, his knuckles white, his concentration intense.

Without warning the big *Frontenac* ground to a sudden stop as she drove up on a rocky reef.

The crew onboard the *Frontenac* all knew the ship was in trouble when they heard the sickening sound of the hull scraping along the rocks. The rumbling and screeching of steel on rock resonated through the ship for what seemed an eternity as the ship drove 150 yards onto the reef before coming to a stop. The ship had driven up on a rocky reef off Pellet Island, south of the shipping channel.

Captain Trueax immediately ordered everyone to put on survival suits and make preparations to launch the lifeboats while an inspection was made of the damage.

After a complete survey of the damage, it was determined that the *Frontenac* was held firmly by the rocks. It was also discovered that the *Frontenac* had sustained severe damage to several bottom plates and water was in the number 3 cargo hold.

An emergency radio call was made to the Reserve Mining Company telling them of their predicament. The mining company boat was sent out to stand by the ship in case an abandon ship order became necessary. Also the Coast Guard station at Duluth, Minnesota dispatched the Cutter Mesquite to Silver Bay to lend assistance.

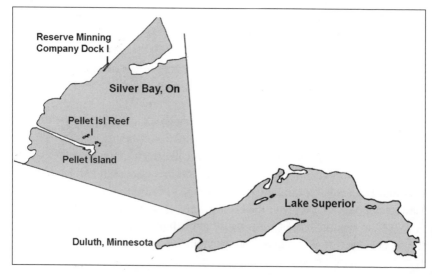

FRONTENAC

The United States Coast Guard Cutter Mesquite. *From the Coast Guard Historians Office.*

Upon its arrival, the crew of the Mesquite placed an oil containment boom around the *Frontenac* in case any of the ship's 47,000 gallons of bunker fuel should leak out and cause an ecological disaster in the bay and surrounding areas. After the storm had subsided, the bunker fuel was transferred to a barge to eliminate the chance of a spill.

Since the *Frontenac* was traveling without cargo, her ballast tanks were full to give the ship stability in the storm. The ballast tanks were pumped out and the ship floated free of the rocks.

Under her own power the *Frontenac* backed off the reef, with the lake water being pumped out of the number 3 cargo hold and the Mesquite standing by, the *Frontenac* made its way to the Reserve Mining Company dock at Silver Bay.

Temporary repairs were made to the ship and, in the company of the tug Peninsula and the steamer Pontiac, the *Frontenac* was moved to Superior, Wisconsin shipyard.

Engineers, shipbuilders, insurance underwriters and company executives inspected the ship and it was determined that the *Frontenac* had been more severely damaged than once thought. The obvious hull damage turned out to be more than 300-feet of her bottom plates torn, punctured, and buckled. In addition there were several undiscovered cracks at the stern.

The committee discussed the damage and it was agreed that the cost to repair 56 year old *Frontenac* exceeded the value of the ship. The *Frontenac* was a total loss.

The Cleveland Cliffs Steamer Pontiac *escorted the Frontenac to Superior, Wisconsin. From the collections of the Port Huron Museum.*

For 56 years the *Frontenac* sailed the lakes delivering her cargo of iron ore, coal and grain to various Great Lake ports. She had been in a couple of scrapes but the rocky reef off Pellet Island did her in. The next time the big *Frontenac* sailed it was to a scrap yard.

SHIPS AT LEAST 600 FEET
JOHN T. HUTCHINSON
AND H. LEE WHITE

The Detroit River, connecting the upper Great Lakes of Michigan, Superior and Huron to Lakes Erie and Ontario is one of the busiest waterways in the nation. The river hosts a fast array of recreational vessels and both freshwater and saltwater commercial traffic.

In the lower portion of the Detroit River lies the river's largest island, Grosse Ile. The Island of Grosse Ile is actually made up of 12 islands covering approximately 18 square miles. It was named by the French; Grosse Ile translates to "Big Island."

Today the island is the home to over 10,000 residents who commute to the mainland across two bridges, the Grosse Ile Toll Bridge and the Wayne County operated "Free Bridge."

The main branch of the Detroit River flows to the east of the island and a narrow Trenton Channel is to the island's west side.

In the late 1800's a railroad bridge was built across the narrow channel to the island and in 1913 a Toll Bridge was constructed.

The Toll Bridge was privately built by Edward W. Voigt, who owned a several hundred acre farm on the island, where he raised draft horses. He used

John T. Hutchinson   **604 Feet in Length**

The John T. Hutchinson. *From the Russel collection of the Port Huron Museum.*

the horses to pull beer wagons for his brewery. Mr. Voigt built the bridge to make it easier to transport the horses to and from the island farm.

The bridge consists of three sections, a 180-foot fixed span from the mainland, a 305-foot swing section and another 180-foot fixed portion to the island. The central section pivots 90 degrees to provide two 125-foot wide channels for the passage for boats.

On August 6, 1965, the 604-foot Great Lakes freighter *John T. Hutchinson* had off loaded a cargo of 12,638 tons of iron ore at the McLouth Steel Corporation south of the Toll Bridge and began its trip up the Trenton Channel.

Captain Williamson, master of the *Hutchinson*, stood on the bridge navigating his ship through the narrow Trenton Channel. As it approached the Toll Bridge, the ship sounded the signal, the traffic gates lowered and the center span of the bridge began to pivot open.

Stopped on the fixed bridge connected to the island were three cars and two trucks waiting for the ship to pass through and the bridge to close. Sitting in their vehicles the drivers watched as the huge ship approached from the south.

The bridge operator watched the ship line up with the passage east of the bridge's pivot. He thought it looked like it was on course to pass through east of the pivot. As he watched, the ship seemed to veer towards the island, almost as if its rudder had failed. The ship's present course put it on a collision course with the east fixed portion of the bridge.

The ship had mechanical difficulties and lost its ability to steer.

The bridge operator began to yell to the drivers of the vehicles to run! Men on the bow of the ship were yelling and waving their arms trying to alert the drivers to get off the bridge. They knew their ship was about to ram the structure.

The Grosse Ile Toll Bridge crossing the Trenton Channel of the Detroit River. From the Grosse Ile Bridge Company.

Captain Williamson sounded the emergency signal and an anchor was dropped trying to slow the forward progress of the ship. The evasive measures were not enough and the bow of the *Hutchinson* rammed into the concrete abutment causing the fixed bridge to topple into the water.

One section of the east fixed span was destroyed, three cars and two trucks were completely or partially submerged but all of the drivers on the bridge had escaped the near death experience and there were not any injuries on the ship.

The *John T. Hutchinson* sustained a 12-foot breach in its starboard bow. The collision bulkhead at the bow of the ship was intact and the ship was not in jeopardy of sinking.

One of the men who was on the bridge at the time of the collision said about the *Hutchinson* bearing down on the bridge; "It loomed so high in the air, it was like a house about to fall on your head!"

Despite the extensive damage to the Grosse Ile Toll Bridge, repairs were made and within months the bridge was again operational.

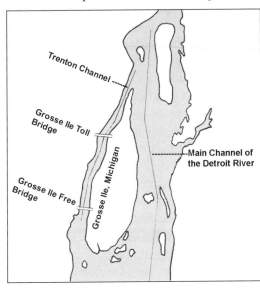

The damage to the Grosse Ile Toll Bridge after the John T. Hutchinson *smashed into it. Photograph from the Grosse Ile, Michigan Historical Society.*

Twenty seven years later history would repeat itself.

On a clear sunny September day the 691-foot long Great Lakes freighter *H. Lee White* was heading south through the Trenton Channel with a 64,000 pound load of iron ore pellets bound for the McLouth steel mill.

The ship, following protocol, radioed the Grosse Ile Toll Bridge the day prior to its arrival to inform them of the approximate time they would be arriving. When over a mile up river the *H. Lee White* met up with two tugboats which would assist the *White* through the narrow Toll Bridge channels, the bridge was again contacted to inform them of the passage.

When in the open position the Grosse Ile Toll Bridge had two channels for ships to pass through, each measuring 125-feet wide. A ship the size of the *H. Lee White* at 78 feet in beam would have less than 24-feet clearance on each side so tugs were necessary to control the ship's side to side movement through the channel.

The tugs and the *White* were traveling south about 5 to 7 miles per hour when they called the bridge operators to tell them they would be at the bridge in 10 to 15 minutes. They received a response assuring the ship that the bridge would be ready for it.

H. Lee White   691 Feet in Length

A photograph of the M/V H. Lee White *approaching the Grosse Ile Bridge on the Trenton Channel. From the Grosse Ile Bridge Company.*

As the tugs and the *White* passed Buoy 28 in the Trenton Channel, the lead tug sounded the required whistle. The bridge did not respond, a second signal was sounded, still with no response and a radio call was made to the bridge. There was no reply.

Customarily as the ship passed Red Buoy 28, 3,000 feet from the bridge, the traffic should have been stopped and the bridge swung opened. When the vessels passed Green Buoy 25 and Red Buoy 26, only 2,000 feet from the bridge, the captain on the lead tug could see the traffic gates had not been lowered and vehicles were still crossing the span. The *H. Lee White* was beyond the point of no return. With the momentum of 64,000 pounds of iron ore in its cargo hold, the ship could not stop in the distance to the bridge.

The lead tug and the *White* began blowing the danger signal, five short blasts on the whistle, to warn the bridge of the ship coming downstream. Cars on the bridge began to stop and it was hoped the bridge would open, but when the master of the White saw two cars start out to cross the span he knew he had to take measures to prevent a collision with the bridge.

Captain Gapcznski quickly radioed the tugs of his intentions then called for the engines to full astern, knowing this action would cause his bow to swing to port. The lead tug moved from the starboard to the port bow to help counter the movement.

The captain watched as the bridge began to open. The *White* continued downriver; 200- to 300-feet from the bridge, Captain Gapcznski ordered the 13,000 pound port bow anchor dropped in an attempt to stop the ship.

The ship slowed as the anchor dragged, finally catching as the bow of the ship gently hit the east end of the fixed bridge. Although the *White* was moving so slowly it barely hit the bridge, the momentum of the ship caused the entire 180-foot structure to fall off its concrete pilings and crash into the water.

In the Coast Guard investigation and legal proceeding that followed the collision of the *White* with the Grosse Ile Toll Bridge, it was found that the two bridge operators on duty on the bridge at the time of the accident were negligent in opening the bridge in a timely manner, thus causing the accident.

The bridge was again repaired and continues to be a vital link for the thousands of Grosse Ile residents to the mainland. Since 1992 there have not been any more incidents.

SHIPS AT LEAST 600 FEET
S.S. ELTON HOYT II AND S.S. ENDERS M. VOORHEES

The 1950's were a great time in American history. The Allies had been victorious in World War II and the economy was flourishing. Practically anyone who wanted a job could find one, and droves of workers headed to the industrial cities in the northern midwest cities to get good paying jobs in the steel mills, automobile factories and other manufacturing plants.

The Interlake Steamship Company steamer the *S.S. Elton Hoyt II* was one of many ships on the Great Lakes carrying record cargos of iron ore from the upper lakes to the industrial complexes on the lower lakes. The ships were meeting the demand for raw materials to feed the need of the booming economy.

On November 23, 1950 the *S.S. Elton Hoyt II* departed South Chicago, Illinois after discharging her cargo of iron ore. The ship, 626-feet in length and 70-feet wide, was steaming light (without cargo) up Lake Michigan bound for Two Harbors, Minnesota.

A late November trip is a challenge to the ships of the Great Lakes for the weather is always unpredictable. A small storm over the Plain States can turn into a beast when it reaches the still relatively warm waters of the lakes.

S.S. Elton Hoyt II   **626 feet in Length**
S.S. Enders M. Voorhees   **622 feet in Length**

The S.S. Elton Hoyt II *steaming down the St. Clair River. From the Russell Sawyer Collection of the Port Huron Museum, Port Huron, Michigan.*

On November 25, 1950, a northwesterly storm had grown in intensity and paralyzed most of the northern half of the nation. On land, the snow was falling at an alarming rate, 10 inches was expected to cover most of Michigan, and the wind reaching as high as 55 miles per hour blew the snow into huge drifts.

On the Great Lakes few ships ventured out. Several ships were anchored in the St. Clair and Detroit Rivers waiting for conditions to improve. Many of the steamers caught out on the lakes sought shelter, while others steamed on through the storm.

One ship that remained out on the lake was the *S.S. Elton Hoyt II.*

The trip up Lake Michigan from South Chicago had been uneventful. As the *Hoyt* passed White Shoal Light in northern Lake Michigan, they recorded in their log that the temperature was sub zero with winds blowing steady at 17 knots and gusting. Snow was falling and the visibility was reduced to one to one and a quarter mile.

The *Elton Hoyt II* was sounding their automatic fog signal in the reduced visibility and Captain George A. O'Boyle was on the bridge throughout the day while the ship steamed along in the snow storm.

As the ship approached the narrow Straits of Mackinaw where Lake Michigan and Lake Huron meet, the captain was told that the radar indicated two ships approaching them on a westerly course. One was off the *Hoyt's* starboard bow, or to the south of the *Hoyt*. The other was off the *Hoyt's* port bow. The ship to port was about ten miles away and the southern ship was closer.

Since the *Hoyt* would pass the vessel to her south first, Captain O'Boyle made a radiotelephone call to the ship. The vessel responded that they were

S.S. ELTON HOYT II AND S.S. ENDERS M. VOORHES

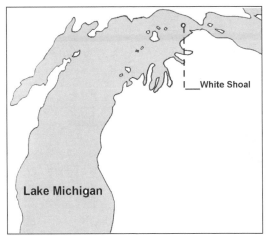

The ships met near White Shoal in upper Lake Michigan.

the *S.S. Enders M. Voorhees*. Captain O'Boyle and second mate of the *Voorhees* conversed and agreed to pass starboard to starboard.

The master of the *Hoyt* altered his course a little to the north to allow for more space between his boat and the *Voorhees* to his south.

The 622-foot *Voorhees*, owned by the Pittsburg Steamship Company of Cleveland, Ohio, had taken on 10,294 tons of iron ore at Two Harbors, Minnesota bound for a steel mill in South Chicago, Illinois.

With reduced visibility due to the snow and other ships in their vicinity, Captain O'Boyle of the *Hoyt* called for half speed, slowing the ship from the full speed it was traveling.

Shortly afterward the *Voorhees'* second mate overheard a radio conversation between the *Hoyt* and the other ship, the Canadian freighter *S.S. Norman B. McPherson*, approaching along with the *Voorhees*. From that discussion, the *Voorhees'* second mate realized that the captain of the *Elton Hoyt II* thought the other vessel was to his north when actually it was the *Voorhees* which was north of their position. The captain of the *Voorhees* immediately tried to establish radio contact with the *Hoyt* to verify the passing arrangements previously made.

Once the confusion as to which ship was north and south of the *Hoyt* was realized, the master of the *Voorhees* called for one whistle, or port to port passing, and ordered his ship to be brought to the south to provide room to pass.

The men on the *Hoyt* bridge looked on in amazement to suddenly see the bow of the *Voorhees* appear about a mile and a quarter off their starboard bow. One whistle blast was heard from the *Voorhees*, indicating they wanted to pass port to port and the ship came to the right .

Captain Nielsen of the *Voorhees* saw the bow of the *Hoyt* appear about 1300-feet away and ordered hard right rudder to bring his ship past the *Hoyt*.

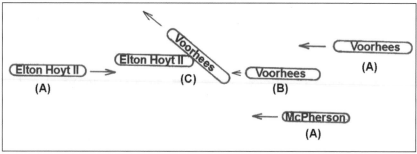

(A) The positions of the three ships when detected on the radar.
(B) The position of the Voorhees *after its course change.*
(C) Point of collision.

Once the bow was beyond the bow of the *Hoyt*, Captain Nielsen ordered hard left rudder in an effort to swing the stern of the *Voorhees* around the *Hoyt*.

Captain O'Boyle on the *Hoyt* also took evasive measures by ordering hard right rudder and full speed astern in hopes to slow his ship and provide room for the *Voorhees* to pass. Three long minutes passed while the two ships continued on, but it became apparent that the ships were closing much too fast and the crews of both ships prepared for the impending collision.

The stem of the *Elton Hoyt II* smashed into the port side of the *Enders M. Voorhees* between number 14 and number 15 cargo hatches.

After the collision, the *Hoyt*, still at full astern, backed away from the *Voorhees*, its bow plates crumbled and badly damaged. However, most of the damage was below the chain locker deck and the undamaged collision bulkhead held back the torrents of cold Lake Michigan water from flooding the ship.

The damage to the *Voorhees* was minimal due to the emergency maneuvering of both masters. Only four hull plates were damaged and a port side tank was ruptured but the cargo hold had not been breached.

After inspections of both ships were completed and neither was found to be in danger of sinking, the *Enders M. Voorhees*, with the *Elton Hoyt II* following, slowly powered to an anchorage near Mackinaw City.

The crews of both ships were very lucky the collision caused minimal damage. If one or both of the ships had gone down and the crews were cast into the lake, they might never have been found in the blinding snow storm.

SHIPS AT LEAST 600 FEET
BUFFALO

Lighthouses on the Great lakes are placed in position for different applications. Some mark the entrance to a harbor. Some are built to guide a ship through a shipping channel and others might be positioned to warn lake traffic to stay clear of a dangerous shoal. The Detroit River lighthouse is located on the west end of Lake Erie where the lake meets the south end of the Detroit River. It warns sailors of the shallow Bar Shoal and marks the turning point for ships entering the river.

The Detroit River is one of the busiest waterways in the world. Any vessel traveling between Lakes Erie and Ontario north to ports on Lakes Michigan, Superior or Huron must pass by the Detroit River light located near the point of the Bar Shoal.

A ship entering the mouth of the Detroit River must make a sweeping turn to the right, taking it near the Bar Shoal which extends from the Canadian shore. After several ships had run aground on the shallow bar and many complaints from mariners, the Canadian Government placed a lightship in the area in 1875.

Lightships have several inherent problems: sometimes they get pushed out of position in high winds and they are prone to high maintenance.

Buffalo   634 Feet in Length

The 634-foot Buffalo. *From the Great Lake photographic collection of Richard Wicklund.*

In such a vital location it became apparent that a permanent structure was needed. The United States government allocated funds for a lighthouse to be built. The structure would warn the mariners of the shoal but also mark the turning point for north bound vessels entering the Detroit River.

A wood crib was assembled at Amherstburg, Ontario and towed to the site where it was filled with concrete and sunk in 22-feet of water. Heavy pieces of granite were delivered by barge and placed on the crib forming a foundation measuring 43-feet wide, 90-feet long and 15-feet high. The foundation is not a rectangle; rather the ends come to a point similar to the bow of a ship. It is shaped in this manor so the spring ice flows will be diverted around the foundation.

The following spring a cast iron light tower was assembled on top of the foundation. The tower is 22-feet in diameter at the base, tapering to an 18-foot diameter at the top. In the 49-foot high

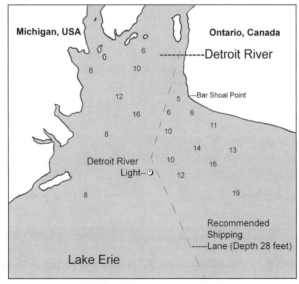

tower there are three decks for crew accommodations, a workroom, a gallery deck and the lantern room. The exact same lighthouse was built at Harbor Beach, Michigan to guide ships into the Harbor of Refuge.

Unlike most lighthouses the light keepers lived in the tower and the one story building next to the tower contained the equipment to operate the fog signal.

An early photograph of the Detroit River Lighthouse. From the United States Coast Guard.

The Detroit River light was an active aid to navigation directing Great Lakes vessels into the Detroit River without major incident until the morning of December 12, 1997. That's the day the lighthouse met the *Buffalo*.

The *Buffalo* is a 634-foot long Great Lakes freighter launched in 1978 from the Bay Shipbuilding Company of Sturgeon Bay, Wisconsin. The ship was the seventh of ten ships launched in the 1970's and early 1980's by the American Steamship Company. The other ships were the 680-foot Roger Keys, the 667-foot Charles E. Wilson, the 704-foot *H. Lee White*, the 634-foot *Sam Laud*, the 770-foot *St. Clair*, the 1,000-foot *Belle River*, the 988-foot *Indiana Harbor*, the 730-foot American Mariner and the 634-foot American Republic.

Being a new ship the *Buffalo* was outfitted with state of the art equipment; both bow and stern thrusters, controllable pitch propellers, and the most current navigational electronics.

The *Buffalo* is no stranger to Great Lake accidents. In the early morning hours of September 12, 1990, the *Buffalo* was on the Saginaw River to deliver a cargo up river. As the freighter passed the tanker Jupiter that was discharging its cargo of gasoline at the Total Petroleum dock, hydrodynamic forces from the *Buffalo* sucked the 383-foot Jupiter from the dock. The movement caused hoses to rupture, ignite the gas and spray flaming gasoline all about the tanker.

The Jupiter was carrying 20,000 gallons of gasoline and burned for 6 days before it was brought under control. One of the Jupiter crew was killed in the accident and the ship was determined to be a total loss.

The Gasoline tanker Jupiter. *From the Great Lakes Photographic collection of Dick Wicklund.*

On December 12, 1997 the *Buffalo* was again involved in another Great Lakes accident. She was running down the Detroit River bound for Cleveland on Lake Erie. The weather was reported to be clear and the seas minimal. The ship's radar was functional, and the *Buffalo* was equipped with technologically advanced electronic navigational equipment, but the 634-foot ship ran almost dead on into the Detroit River Lighthouse.

The thick granite foundation of the lighthouse absorbed the blow of the ship with minimal damage in the collision but the *Buffalo* received a 12-foot gash across its bow.

The ship's bow was damaged and the flooding was restricted to that area. The ship was able to back off the lighthouse foundation and slowly sailed to Toledo where she was laid up for repairs.

What would cause a 634-foot long modern ship to run into a stationary lighthouse; a malfunction of the expensive navigational equipment, using an automatic pilot in the tight confines of a river, limited visibility? The Coast Guard found it to be the result of human error.

A human error that caused $1,200,000.00 damage to the *Buffalo*!

The Jupiter *in flames on the Saginaw River. Photograph courtesy of Jeff and Maureen Martin.*

SHIPS AT LEAST 600 FEET
CARL D. BRADLEY

The wives, children, parents, sweethearts and friends of the crew of the *Carl D. Bradley* anxiously awaited the return of the ship to its home port of Rogers City, Michigan. Of the 35 men of the crew of the *Bradley*, 32 called northern Michigan home, most of them from Rogers City.

The *Carl D. Bradley* was a giant of the Great lakes. At 640-feet in length it was the largest ship on the lakes at the time of its launch on April 9, 1927. She was owned by the Michigan Limestone Division of the U.S. Steel Corporation, and operated by the Bradley line.

The ship was a self-unloading freighter engaged in the transportation of bulk cargo, primarily coal and limestone. The limestone was quarried in Rogers City and other northern Michigan locations and shipped around the Great Lakes to steel mills.

Limestone is used in the productions of steel. Iron ore, coke, (de-gasified coal) and limestone are the main ingredients in the making of steel. Limestone is added to react with and remove the acidic impurities, called slag, from the molten iron. The limestone / impurities mixture float to the top of the molten iron and are skimmed off,

Carl D. Bradley   640 Feet in Length

A painting by Marine Artist Robert McGreevy of the Carl D. Bradley *passing the* Edmund Fitzgerald. *Http://www.mcgreevy.*

During the 1958 season, the *Carl D. Bradley* had completed 43 round trips between the limestone quarries of northern Michigan and steel mills on Lakes Michigan and Erie.

On this last trip of the 1958 season, the *Carl D. Bradley* took on a cargo of 12,000 tons of limestone bound for the U.S. Steel foundry in Gary, Indiana. Captain Roland Bryan, master of the *Bradley* for the last four years, was eager to put this season behind him. The last two years had been tough on the *Carl D. Bradley*.

On April 3, 1956 the *Bradley* was involved in a collision with the *M/V White Rose* on the St. Clair River.

As a result of that collision, the *Bradley* spent part of the 1957 season in drydock for repairs.

In the spring of 1958, while the *Carl D. Bradley* was leaving Port Dolomite near Cedarville, Michigan, she scraped the bottom and received hull damage. After a survey, the owners of the ship determined the damage was minimal and that no repairs were necessary. In November of 1958 the *Bradley* once again scraped bottom while making the turn at Cedarville. In that incident the ship sustained a 14-inch long fracture in its hull. The ship, under its own power, with pumps operating, went directly to Calcite, Michigan (the port at Rogers City) for repairs.

After an inspection, a metal plate was welded over the fracture. Divers were able to complete the repair while the ship remained in the water so a drydock wasn't necessary. Also during the 1958 season, the ship was not in operation from July 1 till October due to a sagging demand for limestone.

Yes, Captain Bryan would be happy to get this season over.

The *Bradley* was in its 31st year on the lakes and it had suffered a collision, two groundings and had millions of tons of cargo pass through its hold. The ship needed a major renovation if its owners wanted to keep her in the fleet.

The Bradley Transportation Fleet had made arrangements with the Manitowoc Ship Building Company of Manitowoc, Wisconsin for an $880,000.00 overhaul during the 1958-1959 winter lay-up. Then once that work was completed, the *Carl D. Bradley* was going to drydock in Chicago for its five-year inspection.

The *Bradley* had discharged its cargo of limestone at Gary, Indiana and on November 17, 1958 and at 10:00 PM pulled away from the dock to return home.

Lake Michigan was relatively calm in view of the 25-35 mile per hour winds that were blowing in from the south. However, the weather forecast predicted the winds to increase to a whole gale (50-65 miles per hour) and shift around to the southwest.

Following company protocol and good judgment, Captain Bryan ordered the ship to be secured for heavy weather. The clamps holding the hatch covers were checked and dogged down tightly. The self-unloading boom received additional lashings to prevent it from coming loose in the impending rough conditions.

The *Bradley* had discharged its cargo and did not have a return cargo so the ship was traveling light. Captain Bryan ordered the forward ballast tanks to be partially filled.

The ballasting of the rear tanks was at the discretion of the Chief Engineer, Ray Buehler. Mr. Buehler had been with the *Bradley* almost since the ship was launched. He knew the engine inside and out; the engine room was his domain.

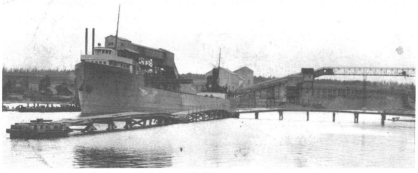

A view of the dock at Calcite, Michigan. From the collections of the Port Huron Musuem.

The Carl D. Bradley. *From the collections at the Bayliss Public Library, Sault Ste. Marie, Michigan.*

The amount of ballast to take on in the aft tanks was determined by the amount of weight needed to keep the propeller and rudder below the surface in rough seas. If a spinning propeller would leave the water on a cresting wave, the propeller spinning freely without the resistance of the water could damage the shaft or engine.

By 4:00 AM, the *Carl D. Bradley* was on a northerly course about eleven miles off Milwaukee, Wisconsin and making about 15 miles per hour. The wind and seas began to increase and the captain ordered the forward ballast tanks to be filled to the maximum.

As the storm increased its rage on the lake, the *Carl D. Bradley* and two other ships, the *S.S. Governor Miller* and the *Richard Trimble* traveled almost parallel courses, although several miles apart, following a northeastern course up Lake Michigan passing Sheboygan and Sturgeon Bay on the Door Peninsula. Also in the area was the foreign ship *M/V Cristian Sartori*.

When the ship was off the Cana Island light, Captain Byant ordered the ship to come to a heading of 046 degrees to cross northern Lake Michigan towards a point between Seul Choix Point and Lansing Shoal.

The first mate of the *Bradley*, Elmer Flemming, went on watch at 4:00 PM. He joined the captain and the helmsmen in the pilothouse. At that time the *Bradley* had passed Poverty Island and the wind was gusting to 60 to 65 miles per hour from the southwest and the waves were a following sea running at 20- to 25-feet. Yet, despite the conditions the *Carl D. Bradley* was riding comfortably.

CARL D. BRADLEY

The Governor Miller. *From the collections of the Port Huron Museum.*

The men on the 4:00 PM watch had eaten dinner prior to coming on watch. Captain Bryan had asked the mess crew to serve it early because he knew when they passed from Lake Michigan into Lake Huron the ship would be taking the waves broadside. An early dinner would allow the cooks an opportunity to clean up and secure everything before they reached Lake Huron.

Most other ships on upper Lake Michigan had sought shelter from the storm behind an island or peninsula or in Green Bay, but such weather didn't send the largest Great Lake freighters to harbor. They usually ignored such weather conditions and plowed through them. The *Carl D. Bradley* had been in conditions worse than this in the past.

Another of the *Bradley* crew, who went on the 4:00 PM watch, was Frank Mays, a 26 year-old deck watchman from Rogers City. During his watch, Mr. Mays checked in at the bridge then walked the length of the ship from the forward house aft. The seas were rough and sometimes breaking on the deck. Then as part of his duties he went below the cargo hold to operate a pump in the sump. He did not find anything alarming, no leaks, or popped rivets. Later during his watch he had occasion to walk the weather deck (An enclosed tunnel below the spar deck used in times of adverse weather) to the engine room. Again he found nothing out of the ordinary.

The Carl D. Bradley *locking through at Sault Ste. Marie. From the State of Michigan Archives.*

The ship continued to ride through the monstrous waves and gale force winds towards the Straights of Mackinaw. The *Bradley* would soon pass into Lake Huron and home to Rogers City. Their expected time of arrival at their home port was 2:00 AM. Wives, girlfriends and children would be waiting up.

At about 5:30 PM, as the ship pounded through the waves a loud, uncharacteristic "Thud" resounded through the *Carl D. Bradley*. It was a sound that when each man heard it knew something was wrong.

Following the "Thud" the men on the bridge reported feeling a vibration, similar to the vibration felt when the propeller was out of the water.

First Mate Flemming looked aft and saw that the stern of the *Carl D. Bradley* was sagging! The ship was breaking up.

Captain Bryan immediately signaled the engine room, on the Chadburn, to stop the engines, then he sounded the abandon ship signal. Elmer Flemming went to the radio on channel 51 and called; "Mayday... Mayday! We are in serious trouble! The ship is breaking up!"

Many shore stations and ships heard the mayday. Further transmissions gave the *Bradley's* position as 12 miles southwest of Gull Island.

Everyone on board knew what they had to do, it was a drill they had practiced regularly. Except this time it wasn't a drill... it was for real. Lifejackets were put on and the crew at the aft of the ship went to their assigned stations, the port and starboard 25 man lifeboats.

At the forward end of the ship the crew mustered at the 15 man life raft stored just aft of the pilot house.

First mate Flemming asked someone to get him a lifejacket but they couldn't find one on the bridge and brought him a life buoy. Mr. Flemming, preferring a lifejacket, completed sending the distress radio call, then ran to his room two decks below the bridge and grabbed his life preserver.

Just minutes after the "Thud" the *Carl D. Bradley* heaved upward and the huge steel ship broke in half!

The break occurred near hatch #10, breaking almost in the middle and leaving two sections each about 300-feet in length.

The broken end of the stern section with lights still aglow swerved to port while the forward section, darkened by the severed electrical cables which ran from the engine room, began to settle at the break.

Lake Michigan's angry waves crashed over the forward section, covering the deck as the section settled. A list developed to port and the forward section of the *Carl D. Bradley* suddenly rolled over and sank.

The crew and the life raft were thrown into the turmoil of wind and huge waves.

The aft section floated on an un-even keel momentarily then it too slipped below the surface. As the aft section sank below the storm tossed surface, steam, a fiery explosion and a large quantity of smoke blasted from the engine room as a result of the cold water reaching the ship's boiler. The lifeboats the crew were making ready for launch were never released from their davits.

The crew of the ship were thrown into the raging lake with waves reaching 25-feet, the height of a two and a half story building. The wind whipped the wave's spray stinging the men's faces as they struggled to keep themselves from slipping below the surface.

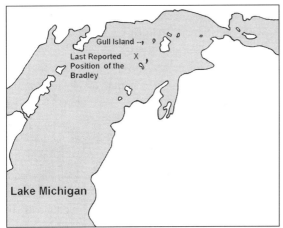

Adding to the men's life and death battle with the lake was the fact that their life jackets were not equipped with a crotch strap and the jackets kept creeping up on them. They had to use one hand to swim and the other to keep from sliding out of the lifejacket. The devise designed to save their lives was actually causing them to expend energy un-necessarily and draining their strength.

The men in the water fought for their lives. The air temperature was 40 degrees and the water temperature of 50 degrees quickly drained them. They rode high on the crest of the twenty five foot waves and were subjected to the 65 mile per hour winds. Next they were cast into the trough of the waves and could see nothing but towering walls of water all around them.

Elmer Flemming luckily surfaced near the six by ten foot life raft and with much effort climbed aboard. Frank Mays was in the raft when it was washed off the ship but was thrown out when the raft was thrust into the sea. He came up about four feet from the raft and frantically swam for it.

They searched for other crewmembers and at first they didn't see anyone but could hear them screaming and hollering.

By chance, the raft was blown near two other crewmen, Gary Strazelecki and Dennis Meredith. Mays and Flemming dragged them onto the raft for a wild ride in the waves and wind.

The closest ship to the *Carl D. Bradley* was the German cargo vessel the *M/V Cristian Sartori*. The *Sartori* was about four miles from the *Bradley* and didn't hear the mayday call but they did see the lights go out in the forward part of the ship followed by an explosion. They immediately altered their course for the *Bradley's* last location. Yet, in the severe sea conditions, it was over an hour and a half before the ship arrived on site.

The United States Coast Guard was also fast to respond to the distress call from the *Bradley*. The Plumb Island and Charlevoix Coast Guard Lifeboat Stations heard the Mayday call and dispatched their rescue boats but the vessels

The 180-foot United States Coast Guard Cutter Sundew. *From the Historian Office of the United States Coast Guard.*

were recalled due to high seas and winds. The vessels, along with that of the Beaver Island station, were put on standby awaiting the conditions to improve.

The Coast Guard Cutter Sundew, stationed at Charlevoix, Michigan quickly got underway and arrived on site at 10:40 PM. A Coast Guard aircraft was returning from an air search on lower Lake Michigan and was called to join in the search for survivors of the *Bradley*. There were two Coast Guard helicopters at the Coast Guard Air Station in Traverse City, Michigan but the prevailing weather prevented them from flying. They were held in readiness for a break in conditions.

Across the lake in Sturgeon Bay, Wisconsin the Coast Guard Cutter Hollyhock made ready and plowed through the waves to the accident site, arriving by 2:30 AM that morning.

The freighter *S.S. Robert C. Stanley* was at anchor at Garden Island when they heard the" Mayday" call. The ship weighed anchor and left the safety of their anchorage to join in the search for survivors of the tragedy.

The *Cristian Sartori* searched through the waves looking for lifeboats, life rafts and crew in life jackets. They searched the violent waters by shining the ships massive search light on the lake. At one time they thought they saw a flare but it disappeared and was not seen again. Captain Mueller, master of the *Cristian Sartori*, reported to the Coast Guard that all they found was a "tank" and a raincoat.

The men clung onto the raft for their lives. At one time their spirits rose when they saw a searchlight from a ship. Elmer Flemming reported that the ships searchlight shone on the life raft momentarily then shut off and the men saw the ship turn away. The "tank" Captain Mueller reported seeing was in fact the life raft!

The four men on the life raft were blown by the wind with each wave threatening to turn it over. After a frightful four hours, a giant wave flipped the raft and tossed the already freezing men into the lake's turmoil. The men expended most of their strength chasing after the life raft and trying to climb back on. Dennis Meredith was too exhausted to swim back to the raft and disappeared in the waves. Two hours later the raft was again tossed end over end by the wind and waves and this time only Flemming and Mays were able to regain the raft.

The two men laid in the life raft clenching the hand lines tied around the upper edge of the raft and prayed. The mountainous waves and ferocious winds, coupled with the cold air temperature, made life for the soaking wet men a living hell.

Presque Isle County Advance EXTRA

Eightieth Year—No. 47 — Rogers City, Michigan — The Limestone City — Thursday, November 20, 1958

STR. BRADLEY SINKS WITH 35 ABOARD

Death Strikes Many Of These Homes

The heavy hand of death lies on the homes of many of these crew members. Never before has the community suffered a loss like this and never has there been such an outpouring of sympathy as for those who have lost their loved ones.

Following are crew members:

Ill-fated Ship Which Sank In Lake Michigan

Community Faces Worst Tragedy In Its History As Death Toll Mounts

Tragedy struck at the hearts and homes of friends and relatives of the thirty-five men aboard the Str. Carl D. Bradley, when the startling news spread quickly throughout the community that the big self-unloader of the Bradley fleet had sunk in Lake Michigan early Tuesday evening.

A dramatic message from Captain Roland Bryan, "The ship is breaking in half, we're going down," was received here in Rogers City by Central Radio and was the first news of impending disaster.

Coast Guard Cutter Sundew Rescues Two From Floating Raft Wednesday Morning

Expression Of Sympathy By Limestone Div. Head

Attendance At Funeral Prevents Possible Death

Ice started forming in Frank Mays' hair and on his coat. This frightened him for he knew if the temperature dropped too much he would freeze to death. He held on to the thought that if they could survive until daybreak they would be found.

A ship searching for any survivors of the *Carl D. Bradley* came within a half of a mile of the raft. The men screamed, waved their arms, tried to light a flare but they were too wet to ignite. Their screams were drowned out by the roar of the wind and they were obscured by the dark of night and heaving waves. The hopes of the men turned to despair as the ship passed into the night.

For six hours the two men had endured the freezing, the wet, the waves, the wind, the loss of their ship, and the loss of their crewmates. They wondered how much more they would be expected to endure.

The Coast Guard ships and civilian vessels searched the rough waters of Lake Michigan, looking for lifeboats and crew who might have survived the sinking of the *Carl D. Bradley*. They had picked up18 bodies floating in lifejackets, but no survivors.

Almost 15 hours after the *Bradley* had broken in two and sunk, the Sundew sighted the life raft 5-1/4 miles east northeast of Gull Island, over 20 miles from where the ship had gone down. The Sundew was maneuvered along side the life raft and a cargo net was thrown over the side. Coast Guard men climbed down and assisted the tired and weak men from the life raft. The two survivors were laid on stretchers, wrapped in blankets and taken to the Chief's quarters where the corpsman performed first aid for hypothermia.

The *Sundew* also sighted a lifeboat from the *Bradley* and recovered it. The boat was empty.

CARL D. BRADLEY

Two men survived the sinking of the *Carl D. Bradley*, 18 bodies were recovered from the lake, and 15 other crewmen were missing and presumed dead. Of the 15 missing all of them were reported to have been on watch in the engine room at the time the *Bradley* broke up.

In a matter of minutes the *Carl D. Bradley*, once the largest ship on the Great Lakes, broke in two pieces and sank to the bottom of Lake Michigan. Of the 35 men onboard only two lived through the ordeal, the first mate Elmer Flemming and deck watchman Frank Mays. The remainder of the crew perished.

Thirty three of the crew lived in Northern Michigan, most from Rogers City, Michigan. The loss of 33 men from such a small geographic area was devastating. There wasn't a person living in Rogers City (population about 4,000 at that time) that wasn't related to or friends with a man killed in the tragedy. The men of the *Carl D. Bradley* left in their wake 25 widows and 54 fatherless children.

In Honor of the Men of the *Carl D. Bradley*

Roland Bryan,	Captain,	Loudonville, New York
Raymond Buehler	Chief Engineer	Lakewood, Ohio
John Zoho	Steward	Claireton, Penn.
John Fogelsonger	Second Mate	St. Ignace, Michigan
Douglas Bellmore	Porter	Onaway, Michigan
Gary Price	Deckhand	Onaway, Michigan
Cleland Gager	Oiler	Onaway, Michigan
Dennis Meredith	Deckhand	Metz, Michigan
Clyde Enos	Stokerman	Cheboygan, Michigan
Alfred Pilarski,	Second Cook	Rogers City, Michigan
Bernard Schefke,	Porter	Rogers City, Michigan
James, Selke,	Porter	Rogers City, Michigan
Paul Greengtske,	Watchman	Rogers City, Michigan
Carl Bartell	Third Mate	Rogers City, Michigan
Joseph Krawczak	Wheelsman	Rogers City, Michigan
Raymond Kowalski	Wheelsman	Rogers City, Michigan
Earl Tulgetske, Jr.	Wheelsman	Rogers City, Michigan
Melville Orr	Watchman	Rogers City, Michigan
Alva Budnick	Watchman	Rogers City, Michigan
Richard Book	Deck Watchman	Rogers City, Michigan
Gary Strzelecki	Deck Watchman	Rogers City, Michigan
Duane Berg	Deckhand	Rogers City, Michigan
John Bauers	First Assistant Eng	Rogers City, Michigan

Alfred Boehmer	2nd Assistant Eng	Rogers City, Michigan
Keith Schular	3rd Assistant Eng.	Rogers City, Michigan
William Elliott	Repairman	Rogers City, Michigan
Dennis Joppich	Wiper	Rogers City, Michigan
Floyd MacDougall	Oiler	Rogers City, Michigan
Paul Horn	Oiler	Rogers City, Michigan
Erhardt Felex	Stokerman	Rogers City, Michigan
Paul Heller	Stokerman	Rogers City, Michigan
Edward Vallee	Conveyorman	Rogers City, Michigan
Leo Promo Jr.	Assistant Convey.	Rogers City, Michigan

Survivors

Elmer Flemming	1st Mate	Rogers City, Michigan
Frank Mays	Deck Watchman	Rogers City, Michigan

(Note: After an exhaustive Coast Guard inquiry into the cause of the sinking of the Carl D. Bradley, *it was determined that damage from the groundings was not the reason the ship broke up. Rather, the ship traveling light in the huge waves caused excessive "hogging" stresses; the forward and aft of the* Bradley *supported on two different waves and the middle of the ship un-supported at the moment of the break.)*

SHIPS AT LEAST 700 FEET
EDMUND
FITZGERALD

Arguably the most well known Great Lakes shipwreck is the *Edmund Fitzgerald*. Newspaper headlines screamed of the loss of the ship. Radio and television spread the news around the world and Gordon Lightfoot's haunting ballad immortalized the loss of the ship.

Most people first learned of the steamer *Edmund Fitzgerald* on November 10, 1975, the day the ship went missing, but to those who love the Great Lakes and freighters, the *Edmund Fitzgerald* was one of the most famous ships on the lakes.

On June 7, 1958 Mrs. Elizabeth Fitzgerald smashed a bottle of champagne on the port bow of hull # 301 and said:

"I christen thee *Edmund Fitzgerald*. God bless you."

The giant ship slid sideways into a yard basin to the blasting of horns and whistles from more that 250 commercial and recreational boats and the cheers of the over 15,000 well wishers gathered to witness the event.

Launched at the Great Lakes Engineering Works yard in River Rouge, Michigan, the *Fitzgerald* was the largest ship to sail the Great Lakes, a distinction the ship carried until 1971 when the 858-foot *Roger Blough* was

Edmund Fitzgerald   **729 Feet in Length**

The Edmund Fitzgerald. *From the Historians Office of the United States Coast Guard.*

launched. The *Fitzgerald* measured 729-feet in length (the length of almost 2-1/2 football fields) and 75-feet across.

The "Big Fitz", as she was affectionately called, was owned by the Northwestern Mutual Life Insurance Corporation of Milwaukee, Wisconsin and joined the growing number of Great Lakes ships in the Northwestern fleet.

The fleet consisted of ships *J. Burton Ayers*, *Joseph S. Wood*, and the *J.H. Hillman Jr.* The Northwestern Mutual Life Insurance Corporation was in the business of investing in Great Lakes commerce, not operating the ships, so the ship *Edmund Fitzgerald* was leased to the Columbia Transportation Division of Oglebay Norton Company of Cleveland, Ohio.

The *Edmund Fitzgerald* was named in honor of the newly elected Chairman of the Board of the Northwestern Mutual Life Insurance Corporation, *Edmund Fitzgerald*.

Mr. Fitzgerald distinguished himself by serving the company for over twenty five years as a Vice President, President and Chairman of the Board. But, Fitzgerald is also a well respected name in Great Lakes maritime history.

Mr. Fitzgerald's father, William Fitzgerald, was the president of the Milwaukee Dry Dock Company which later became known as the American Ship Building Company and William's father, John, and five of his brothers were all captains of Great Lakes sailing vessels.

In Gordon Lightfoot's ballad: "The Wreck of the *Edmund Fitzgerald*," one verse begins:

"The ship is the pride of the American Side…"

EDMUND FITZGERALD

The *Edmund Fitzgerald* truly was the pride of the American side of the Great Lakes for she was the largest ship on the lakes. The "Fitz," one of the many nick names she was affectionately called, carried the largest cargo of any the Great Lakes freighter and she could carry that cargo at a faster speed than any other freighter as well, about 16 MPH.

In addition to her speed and cargo handling capabilities, the ship was also distinguished by her accommodations. They were unsurpassed by any Great Lakes freighter. In the uppermost forward deckhouse, the Texas Deck, was the chart room and the pilot house complete with the newest state of the art electronic communication and navigational equipment. Below on the foc'sle deck was the captain's office and stateroom and private bathroom.

Also on the foc'sle deck were two guest staterooms lavishly furnished by Detroit's J. L. Hudson Company. The guest staterooms were reserved for executives and guests of Oglebay and Norton and the Northwestern Mutual Life Insurance Corporation. There was a large lounge facing aft overlooking the cargo hatches of the ship with a pantry stocked full of drinks and snacks for the pleasure of the guests

Below the foc'sle deck is the weather or spar deck. On this level in the forward deckhouse are found the quarters for the 1st, 2nd, and 3rd mates. Each had a private room with a bathroom. Any unlicensed crew who worked in the pilot house bunked two to a room also on this deck.

Behind the forward deckhouse on the spar deck is the area of a Great Lakes freighter where the cargo hatches are located. On the *Edmund Fitzgerald* there were 21 cargo hatches.

Below the spar deck of the *Edmund Fitzgerald* is a cargo hold of 860,950 cubic feet. This area is divided into three non-water tight areas separated by screened bulkheads. Below the cargo hold and along both sides are the ballast tanks. The ballast tanks took on water for weight to control the ship's trim and to provide weight when the ship was traveling without cargo.

The after deckhouse is located above the engine room and

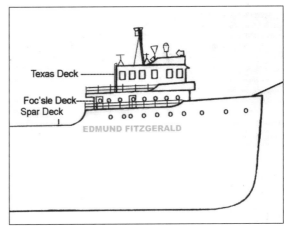

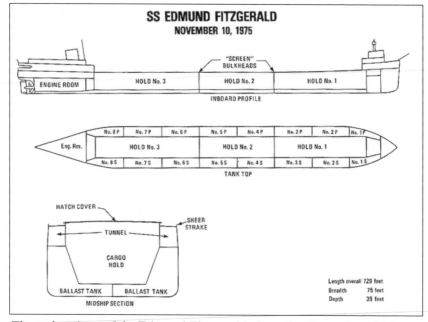

These drawings of the Edmund Fitzgerald, *from the Coast Guard Marine Causality Report, illustrates the location of the three cargo holds, the ballast tanks and the crew passage tunnels below the spar deck.*

contains the crew quarters, a TV room, card room, pool room, the galley and the mess (dining room) and two other dining rooms, one for the officers and the other for guests. Also on this deck, the Chief Engineer maintained an office and a private stateroom. In addition, the 1st, 2nd and 3rd assistant engineers had private rooms. The crew quarters were large as crew accommodations go on Great Lake freighters. All of the non-licensed crew staterooms, each with a private bathroom, were air conditioned and accommodated only two men.

The crew accommodations made the *Edmund Fitzgerald* one of the most sought after assignments on the lakes.

Travel between the after deckhouse and the forward deckhouse was accomplished on the open spar deck in fair weather. In times of high wind or rough seas which would wash a crewmember overboard, travel between the two deckhouses was through two under deck passages or tunnels, which offered protection from the elements.

The 21 cargo hatches of the *Edmund Fitzgerald* had vertical steel walls, or combing, which rose 24 inches above the spar deck. The hatches were covered by 11 x 54 feet long hatch covers made of a single piece of 5/16 inch thick hardened steel. The hatch covers were then held in place by 68 manually tightened Kestner Clamps. To reduce the amount of water that could enter the cargo hold in high seas a gasket around the perimeter of the hatch cover where it met the hatch combing was compressed as the clamps were tightened.

A typical hatch cover and clamps can be seen on this Great Lakes freighter. From the collections of the Port Huron Museum.

The cargo hatches were lifted or replaced with the use of an electrically operated hatch crane. The hatch crane traveled fore and aft on rails mounted on the deck. The crane would be positioned over and made fast to a hatch cover. The operator would activate the crane to raise the heavy hatch cover. The crane would then roll out of the way for loading or unloading of cargo from that hatch.

Once the operation was done, the cargo hatches were replaced and secured down by a crew member manually tightening the Kestner Clamps.

In 1958 when the *Edmund Fitzgerald* was launched, the ship was not only the largest ship on the lakes but also the fastest. The ship impressed all with its speed of 16 MPH.

After her sea trials on September 23, 1958, Captain Lambert, the *Edmund Fitzgerald's* first master, took the ship on her maiden voyage from its River Rouge berth up the Detroit River, through Lake St. Clair and the St. Clair River into the open water of Lake Huron. At Sault Ste. Marie the ship squeezed into the locks with much fanfare, clearing the lock gates with only inches on either side, then sailed into the clear blue waters of Lake Superior.

When the "Big Fitz" returned, she carried a load of taconite pellet which set a record for the largest cargo, by weight, to pass through the Soo Locks, the first of many records the ship would earn throughout her career.

Throughout the 1958 season the "Mighty Fitz" only called on two ports, Silver Bay, Minnesota and Toledo, Ohio. These were the only two Great Lake ports which were large enough to accommodate a ship the size of the *Edmund Fitzgerald*.

During her last trip of the 1958 season the *Fitzgerald* took on a load of taconite pellets in Minnesota and set out into Lake Superior. Captain Lambert was told that weather was building in the Plain States and that it would strike the Great Lakes with vengeance.

The Edmund Fitzgerald *entering the Locks at Sault Ste. Marie, Michigan. From the Bayliss Public Library Collections.*

As the "Mighty Fitz" crossed Lake Superior, the weather held and the ship made good time, but shortly after entering northern Lake Huron the ship was assaulted by 80 mile per hour winds and waves up to 25-feet high. The *Edmund Fitzgerald* was severely battered by the wind and seas causing even veteran sailors to hunker down and question their chosen vocation.

The Edmund Fitzgerald *passing the* Bradley. *A painting by Robert McGreevy, http://www.mcgreevy.com.*

The H. C. Frich *loading iron ore pellets. Note the chutes being lowered to the ship's hatches. From the collections of the Port Huron Museum.*

It wasn't until the ship reached port in Toledo that the crew was informed of the sinking of *Carl D. Bradley* in upper Lake Michigan. The *Bradley's* crew, friends and associates of the men of the *Fitzgerald's* crew, were killed when the *Bradley* broke in two in the same storm that they had just sailed through.

For thirteen years the *Edmund Fitzgerald* held the distinction of being the largest ship on the Great Lakes. During that period the ship set several records for the amount of cargo carried, including in 1964 becoming the first ship to carry one million tons of cargo through the Soo Locks in a single season.

In testament to her designers and engineers, the *Edmund Fitzgerald* remained virtually unchanged during her career. Any changes made were to improve on her performance with technology which was not available at the time of her construction. In 1969 a Byrd-Johnson diesel bow thruster was installed to better control the ship when entering and leaving the Soo Locks and to assist in docking.

The next improvement was the conversion of the main power plant from coal to oil. All of the equipment associated with the coal operation was removed, the new oil fired unit installed and fuel tanks were constructed in the old coal bunkers.

On November 9, 1975 the *Edmund Fitzgerald*, with Captain Ernest McSorley in command, lay moored at the Burlington Northern Railroad Dock

The Edmund Fitzgerald *in better times. From the Historians Office of the United States Coast Guard.*

1 east in Superior, Wisconsin. The "Fitz" took on 50,013 gallons of fuel from a fuel barge which tied up along side as the ship took on its cargo of taconite pellets.

Taconite pellets are produced through a process by which taconite, a form of iron ore, is crushed into a fine powder. The powdered taconite is heated in rotating kilns to form reddish brown balls about one half to five-eights inch in diameter.

The round pellets are easily transported on conveyer belts and railroad hopper cars which discharge from the bottom. The round shape of the pellets also packs more tightly in the cargo hold of a ship than raw iron ore, allowing the ship to carry more cargo.

The cargo loading facility at the Burlington Dock was equipped with storage bins or pockets built high above the deck of a ship. The taconite

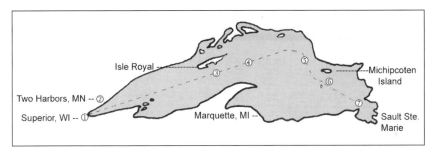

Isle Royal ④ ⑤ Michipcoten Island
Two Harbors, MN -- ② ⑥
Superior, WI -- ① Marquette, MI -- ⑦ Sault Ste. Marie

pellets were loaded into hopper cars which were pushed by a locomotive up on top of the dock and located over the pockets. Once in position the bottom of the hopper car was opened and the pellets fell into the pockets.

To load a ship like the *Edmund Fitzgerald*, the ship would be moored along side the dock with its cargo hatches aligned with the loading chutes on the dock. The chutes would be lowered into the cargo hatches, a gate lifted and the taconite pellets would roll down into the hold of the ship.

The cargo was loaded into the ship under the direction of the chief mate. It was his responsibility to maintain the ship's trim and draft while loading. He directed the pumping out of ballast water while the cargo was loaded so the ship remained on an "Even Keel".

At approximately 7:30 AM on November 9, 1975, the *Edmund Fitzgerald* was moored starboard side to the dock. The pockets had been filled earlier and the procedure began.

The first chute to be lowered and discharged was into cargo hatch number 21, the hatch furthest aft. A load of approximately 300 tons poured into the hold of the *Fitzgerald*.

The ship was then shifted aft twelve feet so the next chute was aligned with hatch number 20.

This filling of taconite pellets, the pumping out of ballast water and the moving to align with the chutes continued until 1:15 PM. By then the *Fitzgerald* had taken on a cargo of 26,116 tons of cargo to be delivered to the steel mill at Zug Island in the Detroit River.

Once loaded with the taconite pellets the crew of the *Edmund Fitzgerald* readied the ship to depart Superior, Wisconsin.

The trip would cover approximately 750 miles, taking the ship across the length of Lake Superior, through the locks at Sault Ste. Marie, down the St. Marys River into northern Lake Huron, over 200 miles down the length of Lake Huron into the St. Clair River and Lake St. Clair finally to Zug Island on the Detroit River. For the *Edmund Fitzgerald* it would be a 5-day trip.

The Arthur M. Anderson. *From the collections of the Port Huron Museum.*

On November 9, 1975 at approximately 2:15 PM the "Mighty Fitz" steamed away from the Burlington Docks in Superior, Wisconsin. The ship, at full speed, assumed the recommended course to transit Lake Superior.

After two hours, the *Fitzgerald* was off Two Harbors, Minnesota where the Great Lakes freighter *Arthur M. Anderson* of the United States Steel Corporation, was departing with a cargo of taconite pellets en route to Gary, Indiana.

The captain of the *Anderson*, Jesse Cooper, received a radio transmission from the National Weather Service announcing they had posted gale warnings for Lake Superior. Sighting a ship several miles to the southwest of his position, Captain Cooper radioed the ship.

Cooper: "W4805, *Arthur M. Anderson* to the vessel northbound abeam Knife River. Do you read me?"

McSorley: "*Anderson* this is the *Edmund Fitzgerald*. Over"

Cooper: "This is the *Anderson*. Have you picked up the gale warnings the Weather Service just posted?. Over."

McSorley: "This is the *Fitzgerald*, ah, roger."

Cooper: "I'm thinking I will take the northern track; get over to the north shore for shelter in case it really starts to blow. Over."

McSorley: "I've been thinking the same thing. I'm steering sixty-five degrees for Isle Royale."

Captains Cooper and McSorley elected to abandon the more direct southern course across the lake for a course which would take them more towards the northern shore of Lake Superior. It was not uncommon for lake vessels to use the northern route and let the Canadian land mass provide shelter. The two ships agreed to travel the same course.

On November 8, a meteorological disturbance developed over the Oklahoma Panhandle. At that time it was expected to become a typical fall storm and pass south of Lake Superior. But by 9:00 AM on November 9, a new prediction had the storm crossing the eastern end of Lake Superior on up into Canada.

Ten hours later, at 7:00 PM the National Weather Service issued a gale warning for the lake, meaning winds from 40 to 52 miles per hour were expected.

Some Great Lake ships are local weather reporters. They call in at 1:00 AM, 7:00 AM, 1:00 PM and 7:00 PM giving their position and relating the weather at their location. Both the *Anderson* and *Fitzgerald* participated in this program.

The *Edmund Fitzgerald* provided a weather report on November 10 at 1:00 in the morning. The *Fitzgerald* reported the winds at 60 miles per hour from the north northeast and the waves were running at 10-feet. Their location at the time was 20 miles south of Isle Royale.

An hour later, the National Weather Service issued a storm warning with expected winds in excess of 60 miles per hour and up to 15-foot seas. The captains of both ships knew they would be in for a long night on Lake Superior

The faster *Fitzgerald* passed the *Anderson* as the two ships made their way through the horrendous conditions. On shore, a 60 mile per hour wind could

The Edmund Fitzgerald *passing through the St. Clair River. From the Great Lakes photograph collection of Hugh Clark.*

uproot trees, and do structural damage to buildings. On a ship in the middle of Lake Superior, the winds would easily blow a man overboard and anything not securely bolted down would be ripped from the ship. The wind was horrible and the huge wind whipped waves crashed on the ships covering their deck with cascading torrents of water with enough force to wash anything overboard.

At 7:00 AM on November 10, the *Edmund Fitzgerald* reported its position as 35 miles north of Copper Harbor, Michigan on the tip of the Keweenaw Peninsula. Ten foot waves were pounding the ship and 40 + mile per hour winds blasted the ship.

Five hours later when the ships had traveled about 60 miles since the last report, the *Anderson* radioed in a weather report. The winds were from the southeast at approximately 23 miles per hour with waves at 12-feet. Their position was 20 miles northwest of Michipicoten Island. The *Fitzgerald* did not issue a weather report, but the *Anderson* had her position as 11 miles northwest of the island.

Captains Cooper and McSorley communicated about the course they would follow along the Canadian shore southeast towards the locks at Sault

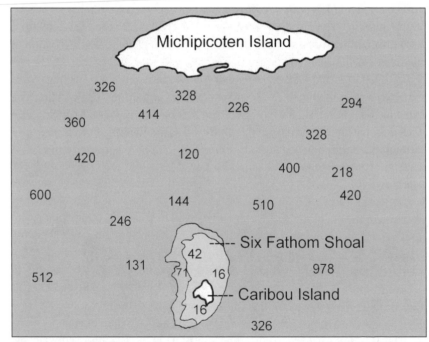

The shallow Six Fathom Shoal surrounds Caribou Island. The numbers in the drawing represent depths in feet.

Ste. Marie. The master of the *Anderson* elected to head west a bit to pass clear of Michipicoten Island. Captain McSorley responds:

McSorley: "Well, I am rolling some, but I think I'll hold the course until I'm ready to turn for Caribou."

At 3:15 PM the *Edmund Fitzgerald* changed its course to pass between Caribou Island and Michipicoten Island. On the bridge of the *Arthur Anderson*, Captain Cooper watched the *Fitzgerald's* course on the radar. He called first mate, Morgan Clark, to take a look. They discussed how close the *Fitzgerald* was to Six Fathom Shoal. Captain Cooper remarked that they were in closer than he would want his ship to be.

The Six Fathom Shoal is a shallow rocky shoal surrounding Caribou Island. The island, approximately 3.5 miles north to south and less than 1.5 miles across, is located 21 miles south of Michipicoten Island. Between the islands the water is several hundred feet deep but the shoal surrounding the island has depths from 42- to 16-feet.

About 3:30 PM, Captain McSorley called Captain Cooper.

McSorley: "*Anderson* this is the *Fitzgerald*. I have sustained some topside damage. I have a fence rail laid down, two vents lost or damaged, and a list. I'm checking down. Will you stay by me till I get to Whitefish?"

Cooper: "Charlie on that *Fitzgerald*. Do you have your pumps going?"

McSorley: "Yes, both of them."

By checking down, Captain McSorley meant he was going to reduce the *Fitzgerald* so the *Anderson* could catch up with them. At that time the *Fitzgerald* was about 15 miles ahead of the *Anderson*. The ships were heading for Whitefish Bay on the southeast shore of Lake Superior. There they could anchor in the bay and wait out better weather to continue on to the Soo Locks.

The *Edmund Fitzgerald* was fitted with several vents. The port and starboard access tunnels had vents fore and aft. Each ballast tank was also equipped with a vent. If the vents were damaged or lost, lake water would pour in through the openings. The water then would be removed by the pumps.

The ship was equipped with four 7,000 gallon per minute ballast pumps and two 2,000 gallon per minute auxiliary pumps.

Forty minutes later Captain McSorley contact the *Anderson* by radio.

McSorley "*Anderson*, this is the *Fitzgerald*. I have lost both radars. Can you provide me with radar plots till we reach Whitefish Bay?"

Cooper: "Charlie on that, *Fitzgerald*. We'll keep you advised of your position."

The *Edmund Fitzgerald* is heading southeast in the storm tossed waters of Lake Superior. The ship has sustained damage and has a list to starboard.

The Arthur M. Anderson. *From the Hugh Clark Great Lakes Photographic collection.*

Hurricane force winds beat down on her and waves as high as a two and half story building are mounting the ship from her stern and washing over her decks. Now both radars are inoperable.

The radar didn't work but the *Fitzgerald* was equipped with a radio directional finder (RFD). An RDF is an electronic devise which determines the direction a radio signal is coming from. The Coast Guard maintained stations around the Great Lakes to transmit radio signals for ships to pick up and plot their position. The *Fitzgerald* was trying to pick up the signal from Whitefish Point so they could set a course to Whitefish Bay.

Unable to pick up the signal from Whitefish Point, Captain McSorley radioed the Coast Guard at Grand Marais to check if the radio beacon was functional. Both the Whitefish Point radio beacon and the lighthouse had been knocked out by the storm.

The *Edmund Fitzgerald* had no radar and it couldn't pick up the Whitefish Point radio beacon, the ship is traveling blind. The *Fitzgerald* had to depend on the *Anderson* to guide it to the safety of Whitefish Bay.

Between 5:30 and 6:00 PM, Captain Cedric, a Great Lakes Pilot aboard the Swedish ship *Avafors* established radio communication with the *Fitzgerald*.

Cedric: "*Fitzgerald*, this is the *Avafors*. I have the Whitefish light now but still am receiving no beacon. Over."

McSorley: " I'm very glad to hear it."

Cedric: "The wind is really howling down here. What are the conditions where you are?"

Captain Cedric overhears Captain McSorley shouting at someone on the *Fitzgerald*:

McSorley: "Don't let nobody on deck! (unintelligible) "…vents"

Cedric: "What's that, *Fitzgerald*? Unclear. Over."

McSorley: "I have a bad list, lost both radars. And am taking heavy seas over the deck. One of the worst seas I've ever been in."

Cedric: "If I'm correct, you have two radars."

McSorley: "They're both gone."

The *Anderson* was buffeted by the horrifying winds, gusting in excess of 100 miles per hour, snow squalls and tremendous waves, running 16- to 26-feet, as it traveled towards the protection Whitefish Bay offered. It was making up time on the *Fitzgerald* which was now only 10 miles ahead of her position.

Captain Jesse Cooper, reported sometime before 7:00 PM the *Anderson* was assaulted by two immense waves. The waves covered the ships spar deck with green water to a depth of 12-feet, making the wave, he estimated, over 35-feet in height!

The wave crashed down on the stern of the *Anderson* with such force that aft the lifeboat, sitting on a saddle, was forced down leaving an impression of the saddle in the metal of the lifeboat.

The two waves far exceeded the average waves on the lake for that time period. A wave or waves higher than the predominate waves are not uncommon on the lakes. Called a rogue wave, they travel along the surface of the lake combining with other waves, absorbing their energy and mounting in height.

First mate Clark, on the *Anderson*, sights a north bound ship on the radar ahead of the *Fitzgerald* and radios them at 7:10 PM to relay the information.

Clark: "*Fitzgerald*, this is the *Anderson*. Have you checked down?"

McSorley: "Yes, we have."

Clark: *Fitzgerald*, we are about 10 miles behind you, and gaining about 1-1/2 miles per hour. *Fitzgerald*, there is a target 19 miles ahead of us. So the target would be 9 miles on ahead of you."

McSorley: "Well, am I going to clear?"

Clark: "Yes. He is going to pass to the west of you."

McSorley: "Well, fine."

Clark: "By the way, *Fitzgerald*, how are you making out with your problems?"

McSorley: "We are holding our own."

Clark: "Okay, fine. I'll be talking to you later."

At times the lights of the *Fitzgerald* could be seen from the *Anderson* in the distance. But shortly after the transmission, the lights of the *Fitzgerald* were obscured by a snow squall.

Ten minutes later the squall cleared. The men on the bridge of the *Anderson* could see the lights of three up-bound vessels but not the lights of the *Fitzgerald*.

Captain Cooper checked the *Anderson's* radar. There was no sign of the *Fitzgerald*. Moments later a target is seen on the radar but it disappears.

The *Anderson* attempts to call the *Fitzgerald* on the radio. There wasn't an answer. He called a "saltie" in the area, still no reply. Could the storm have blown out the *Anderson's* radio and it isn't transmitting? To check Captain Cooper calls the steamer *William Clay Ford*. They receive and respond. The radio works, it's the *Fitzgerald* that isn't receiving or transmitting.

At 7:39 PM the *Anderson* calls the Sault Ste. Marie Coast Guard to report they cannot locate the *Fitzgerald* visually, by radar or by radio.

They again contact the Coast Guard at 7:55 PM to inform them that they had lost communication and sight of the *Fitzgerald*.

At 8:32 PM Captain Cooper again calls the Coast Guard;

Cooper: "Soo Control, this is the *Anderson*. I am very concerned about the welfare of the steamer *Edmund Fitzgerald*. He was right in front of us, experiencing a little difficulty. He was taking on a small amount of water and none of the upbound ships have passed him. I can see no lights as before and I don't have him on radar. I just hope he didn't take a nose dive!"

Soo Control: "This is Soo Control. Roger. Thank you for the information. We will try and contact him. Over."

At 9:00 PM Coast Guard Group Soo makes a call to the *Arthur Anderson*.

Group Soo: "*Anderson*, this is Group Soo. What is your position?"

Captain Cooper: "We're down here, about two miles off Parisienne Island right now ...the wind is northwest forty to forty-five miles here in the bay."

Group Soo: "Is it calming down at all, do you think?"

Captain Cooper: "In the bay it is, but I heard a couple of salties talking up there, and they wish they hadn't gone out."

Group Soo: "Do you think there is any possibility that you could ...ah ...come about and go back there and do any searching?"

Coast Guard Station Sault Ste. Marie did not have a vessel available that could go out in the lake with the wind and wave conditions on Lake Superior.

Captain Cooper: "Ah... God, I don't know... that... that sea out there is tremendously large. Ah... if you want me to, I can, but I'm not going to be making any time: I'll be lucky to make two or three miles an hour going back out that way."

The *Anderson* had just gone through hell to get to the safety of Whitefish Bay, and now Captain Cooper was being asked to put his ship and crew in jeopardy to go back out into the howling wind and 16- to 25-foot seas to look for the *Edmund Fitzgerald* or possibly her crew in lifeboats or life rafts.

Group Soo: "Well, you'll have to make a decision whether you will be hazarding your vessel or not, but you're probably one of the only vessels right now that can get to the scene. We're going to try to contact those saltwater vessels and see if they can't possibly come back also... things look pretty bad right now; it looks like she may have split apart at the seams like the *Morrell* did a few years back."

All three of the saltwater vessels told the Coast Guard that they didn't think they could come about due to the severity of the conditions.

Captain Cooper: "Well, that's what I been thinking. But were talking to him about seven and he said that everything was going fine. He said that he was going along like an old shoe; no problems at all."

Group Soo: "Well, again do you think you could come about and go back and have a look in the area?"

Captain Cooper: "Well, I'll go back and take a look, but, God, I'm afraid I'm going to take a hell of a beating out there... I'll turn around and give it a whirl, but God, I don't know. I'll give it a try."

Group Soo: "That would be good..."

Captain Cooper: "You do realize what the conditions are out there?"

There isn't an immediate response from Coast Guard Group Soo.

Captain Cooper: "You do realize what the conditions are out there, don't you?

Group Soo: "Affirmative. From what your reports are I can appreciate the conditions. Again, though, I have to leave that decision up to you as to whether it would be hazarding your vessel or not. If you think you can safely

The Hilda Marjanne. *From the Hugh Clark Great Lakes Photograph collection.*

go back up to that area, I would request that you do so. But, I have to leave the decision up to you."

Captain Cooper: "I'll give it a try, but that's all I can do."

The Coast Guard Air Station at Traverse City had a fixed wing HU-16 aircraft in the air within 30 minutes while the Group Soo 110-foot harbor tug, Naugatuck, went to Whitefish Bay but was ordered not to go into the lake. Coast Guard regulations prohibited the Naugatuck from operating in conditions when winds are in excess of 60 miles per hour.

There were other ships at anchor in the safety of Whitefish Bay; the *William Clay Ford, Hilda Marjanne, William R. Roesch, Benjamin F. Fairless, Frontenac, Murray Bay* and *Algosoo*. The Coast Guard requests them to go back into the lake and search for the missing *Fitzgerald* or survivors of her crew. Only the 629-foot *William Clay Ford* and the 504-foot *Hilda Marjanne* agreed to venture out into the tempest and search for their fellow sailors.

The wind was blowing in excess of 50 miles per hour with gusts much higher, as the ships plowed into the huge waves slowly making their way towards the last known position of the *Fitzgerald*. After a short time the captain of the smaller Hilda Marjanne determined the conditions were too much for his vessel and had to return to Whitefish Bay.

The *William Clay Ford* and the *Arthur M. Anderson* searched throughout the night. As the conditions dissipated the two ships are joined by the *Armco, Roger Blough, Reserve, Wilfred Sykes, William R. Roesch, Frontenac, Joan O. McKellar,* and the *Murray Bay*.

Aiding in the search from the air there were C-130 from the Air National Guard, a Canadian Coast Guard C-130 and three helicopters from the Coast Guard Air Station at Traverse City, Michigan.

The William Clay Ford *went out into the storm to search for the* Fitzgerald. *From the collections of the Port Huron Museum.*

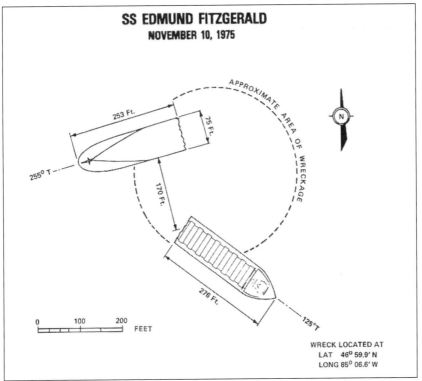

The wreckage of the Edmund Fitzgerald *as it lies on the bottom of Lake Superior. From the Coast Guard Marine Causality Report.*

The ships and aircraft searched the eastern end of Lake Superior throughout the night and for the next few days. All that was found from the *Edmund Fitzgerald* was a lifeboat, half of another, two inflatable life rafts, twenty one life jackets or pieces of them, other pieces of flotsam... No ship, no survivors, no bodies.

On November 16, 1975, two large objects laying close to one another were found on the bottom of Lake Superior. Successive sonar searches and photographs taken by an unmanned remotely operated submarine verified the targets on the bottom were indeed the *Edmund Fitzgerald.*

The *Fitzgerald* lays in approximately 530-feet of water, at a position of 46.59.9 N, 85.06.6 W. just in Canadian water, seventeen miles northwest from the safety of Whitefish Point. The 729-foot ship was broken in two parts; a 276-foot bow section in an upright position with the stern section lying upside-down at an angle to the bow section. An approximately 200-foot

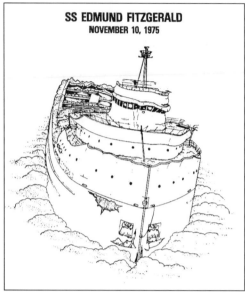

SS EDMUND FITZGERALD
NOVEMBER 10, 1975

The bow section of the Edmund Fitzgerald *as it appears on the bottom. From the Coast Guard Marine Causality Report.*

long mid section was reduced to pieces and lies within the wreck site.

In the weeks, months and years that followed the sinking, the *Edmund Fitzgerald* was the subject of investigations by many organizations including the Coast Guard Marine Board of Investigation, The National Transportation Safety Board and the Lakes Carriers' Association. Theories of what caused the *Edmund Fitzgerald* to sink are plentiful and range from the plausible to the absurd. But, they are all just theories. There is not a definitive answer, as of yet, as to the cause of the loss.

The Coast Guard Marine Board came to the conclusion that the cause of the sinking of the *Edmund Fitzgerald* was due to massive flooding of the cargo hold. They based this on their observation of un-damaged cargo hold clamps.

The Coast Guard underwater photographs revealed some of the hatch clamps to be bent and distorted from the stress of the hatch covers being ripped off during the ship's plunge and impact with the bottom of the lake.

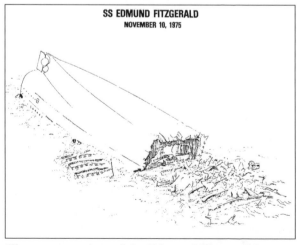

SS EDMUND FITZGERALD
NOVEMBER 10, 1975

The stern section of the Edmund Fitzgerald. *From the Coast Guard Marine Causality Report.*

Yet many hatch clamps were un-damaged, leading to the conclusion of the Coast Guard that many of the hatch clamps were not properly adjusted and worked loose or were not latched down in the first place. They based this assumption on the proposition that if the clamps were properly tightened down before the ship sunk they should be distorted after the accident.

If the hatch clamps were not in place or improperly adjusted, lake water could gain access to the cargo hold. Since the three cargo holds were separated by a screen rather than watertight bulkheads, the water could migrate throughout the ship.

This theory is based on evidence shown on the photographs but many first hand reports from men who had sailed on the *Fitzgerald* said that Captain McSorley would never had permitted the *Fitzgerald* to leave port without the hatch covers being properly secured. They said that some of the clamps were damaged and did not work but there were more than enough which did function correctly.

Another widely accepted theory of the cause of the sinking of the *Fitzgerald*, one that the Lake Carriers' Association supports, is that the ship struck bottom and was damaged while crossing Six Fathom Shoal.

Captain Cooper of the *Arthur Anderson* testified that he observed the *Fitzgerald* on the radar and he stated to his mate that the ship was closer to Six Fathom Shoal than he would want his ship to be.

While the lake is several hundred feet deep between Michipicoten and Caribou Islands, the shallow rocky reef surrounding Caribou extends almost five miles to the north with depths less than 40-feet. A ship in waves of 16- to 25-feet or greater could easily scrape the bottom in shallow water while the ship was in the trough of the waves.

A painting by Marine Artist Robert McGreevy of the Edmund Fitzgerald *on the bottom of Lake Superior. Http://www.mcgreevy.com.*

An underwater photograph of the stern of the Edmund Fitzgerald. *From the Historian office of the Coast Guard.*

It is possible that the *Fitzgerald* came too close to the shoal and grounded causing bottom plates to rupture and allowing water to enter the ballast tanks. Possibly Captain McSorley thought the water in the ballast tanks was coming from the missing vents when actually it was from the vents and from the damaged bottom. The pumps could not remove the water fast enough and the ship would take on a list and eventually lose its buoyancy and sink.

While this is a valid theory, the upside-down stern section does not show any evidence, scratches or punctures, of it scrapping along the rocky shoal and subsequent dives on the Six Fathom Shoal do not show any recent scrapes.

Captain Cooper told of two approximately 35-foot waves which were much larger than the storms predominate waves. He holds to the theory that the two rogue waves hit the *Fitzgerald* on the stern and covered the entire spar deck with several feet of water. This water raced forward along the spar deck of the ship crashing to a stop and mounting at the forward deckhouse. The extra weight of the water so far forward on the ship forced the bow down and the ship could not recover quickly enough to rise with the next wave. Instead the *Edmund Fitzgerald* dove below the surface of Lake Superior until it struck and broke up on the bottom.

Some people theorize that the *Edmund Fitzgerald* broke apart on the surface before she dove to the bottom. They point to the fact that in a storm with large waves a ship the length of the *Fitzgerald* might have been subjected to stress fractures in her hull.

The fractures could have occurred as the hull flexed while riding the huge waves. A 729-foot ship such as the *Fitzgerald* is not fully supported along its

The Edmund Fitzgerald. *From the collections of the Port Huron Museum.*

entire length in large waves, rather a wave might be under the forward section of the ship and the next wave might be towards the stern leaving the center unsupported. Possibly the next wave might support the center while the bow and stern sections are unsupported. This flexing of the hull could result in stress fractures which lead the ship to break apart.

There is a small element that believes that the loss of the *Edmund Fitzgerald* was the result of an alien encounter. This theory is not credible, is absurd and a dishonor to the *Fitzgerald's* crew who lost their lives.

Whatever happened on that night of November 10, 1975 it occurred quickly, the ship never had time to radio a distress call.

A definitive cause of the sinking of the 729-foot *Edmund Fitzgerald* has not yet been discovered and it might never be. There are not any eye witnesses who can tell of the last few hours and minutes of the ship's existence. Most of what is known is from the radio transmissions between the *Fitzgerald* and the *Anderson* and other ships, but the communications are void of details. The remains of the ship provide some clues but there are still more questions than answers.

What is known for sure is that the *Edmund Fitzgerald* departed Superior, Wisconsin with a load of 26,116 tons of iron ore pellets, a crew of 29 men and the ship never arrived. The wreckage of the ship has been found but the men are still listed as missing.

In Honor of the Crew of the *Edmund Fitzgerald*

Ernest M. McSorley,	63	Captain	Toledo Ohio
John H. McCarthy,	62	Mate	Bay Village, Ohio
James A. Pratt,	44	Sec. Mate	Lakewood, Ohio
Michael E. Armagost,	37	Third Mate	Iron River, Wisconsin
Thomas Bentsen,	23	Oiler	St. Joseph, Michigan
Thomas D. Borgeson,	41	Maint. Man	Duluth, Minnesota
John D. Simmons,	60	Wheelsman	Ashland, Wisconsin
Eugene W. O'Brien,	50	Wheelsman	St. Paul, Minnesota
John J. Poviach,	59	Wheelsman	Bradenton, Florida
Ranson E. Cundy,	53	Watchman	Superior, Wisconsin
William J. Spengler,	59	Watchman	Toledo, Ohio
Karl A. Peckol,	20	Watchman	Ashtabula, Ohio
Mark A. Thomas,	21	Deck Hand	Richmond Heights, Ohio
Paul M. Riippa,	22	Deck Hand	Ashtabula, Ohio
Bruce L. Hudson,	22	Deck Hand	North Olmsted, Ohio
David E. Weiss,	22	Cadet	Agoura, California
Robert C. Rafferty,	62	Steward	Toledo, Ohio
Allen G. Kalmon,	43	Sec. Cook	Washburn, Wisconsin
Frederick J. Beetcher,	56	Porter	Superior, Wisconsin
Nolan F. Church,	55	Porter	Silver Bay, Minnesota
George J. Holl,	60	Chief Eng.	Cabot, Pennsylvania
Edward F. Bindon,	47	1st Asst. Eng.	Fairport Harbor, Ohio
Thomas E. Edwards,	50	2nd Asst. Eng.	Oregon, Ohio
Russell G. Haskell,	40	3rd Asst. Eng.	Millbury, Ohio
Oliver J. Champeau,	41	3rd Asst. Eng .	Milwaukee, Wisconsin
Blaine H. Wilhelm,	52	Oiler	Moquah, Wisconsin
Ralph G. Walton,	58	Oiler	Fremont, Ohio
Joseph W. Mazes,	59	Maintenance	Ashland, Wisconsin
Gordon F. MacLellan,	30	Wiper	Clearwater, Florida

(Authors Note: For a complete and detailed account of the history, career and sinking of the Edmund Fitzgerald *I highly recommend; "The Wreck of the* Edmund Fitzgerald*" by Frederick Stonehouse. (Published by Avery Color Studios.)*

SHIPS AT LEAST 700 FEET
MONTCLIFFE HALL, CARTIERCLIFFE HALL AND STEELCLIFFE HALL

Most ships sailing the Great Lakes were built on the lakes. There are the foreign ships (nicknamed "Salties") that sail in and out of the lakes, but most of the ships that stay in the lakes were built in the region. An exception to this are the *Cartiercliffe Hall*, *Steelcliffe Hall* and the *Montcliffe Hall*.

The ships were built by Schlieker-Werft, in Hamburg, West Germany in 1959. All three ships, 546-feet in length and 73-feet in beam, were constructed to transport iron ore between the mines in Venezuela and the steel manufacturers of Europe.

The ships were of a type designed to operate on the ocean, a sharply raked bow with the pilothouse located amidship.

Three of the ships named the *Ems Ore*, *Ruhr Ore* and the *Rhine Ore* prospered in the role until 1976 when they were sold to Hall Corporation Shipping Ltd. of Montreal, Canada to carry iron ore from Gulf of St. Lawrence ports to steel mills at Hamilton, Ontario.

The Hall Corporation sent the vessels to the shipyard to change their design. The ships had their bow removed and a new foreword section was installed lengthening the vessel from 546- to 730-feet. The mid-ship

Montcilffe Hall / Cartiercliffe Hall / Steelcliffe Hall
730 Feet in Length

The Montcliffe Hall *wintering in Sarnia, Ontario after a fire in its deck house. Photograph from the collection of the Port Huron Museum.*

pilothouse and cabins were remodeled and moved aft. The alterations gave the ship a cargo carrying capacity of 29,518 tons.

The *Ems Ore* was renamed *Montcliffe Hall*, the *Ruhr Ore* became the *Cartiercliffe Hall* and the *Rhine Ore* was renamed the *Steelcliffe Hall*. In 1977 they began the next phases of their careers.

The morning of June 5, 1979 found the *Cartiercliffe Hall* about 10 miles off Michigan's Keweenaw Peninsula in Lake Superior. The ship had taken on a cargo of grain at Duluth, Minnesota bound for Port Cartier, Quebec. About 5:00 AM, a fire broke out in the engine room. The fire spread quickly throughout the aft end of the ship filling the passageways and rooms with thick suffocating smoke.

As the smoke filled the bridge, the wheelman sounded the general alarm, stopped the engine and made a "Mayday" call before he had leave.

Crewmen in their cabins could not leave through the smoke filled passageways, they crawled out through portholes and were pulled to safety to the deck above.

Nineteen of the 25 man crew escaped the burning ship in life rafts, six bodies were later found trapped in the engine room. Most survivors suffered from burns, smoke inhalation and shock. Many were hospitalized, with four flown to the University of Michigan Burn Center.

The two Great Lakes freighters, *Thomas Lamont* and *L. R. Desmarais* responded to the Mayday call and took on the survivors from the life rafts. The injured were cared for until they were taken ashore by Coast Guard boats and helicopters.

The ship was towed to Thunder Bay, Ontario where the bodies of the men trapped in the engine room were removed and the Canadian and United States Coast Guards began an investigation into the fire.

An estimate of $4,500,000.00 of damage was done to the *Cartiercliffe Hall* but after an extensive rebuild the ship again sailed the lakes.

Since the fire on the *Cartiercliffe Hall*, changes were made to her two other ships. In 1980 a firewall was installed in the *Montcliffe Hall* to prevent a fire from spreading so quickly as had happened during the blaze on the *Cartiercliffe Hall*. During the 1981 winter lay-up, the *Montcliffe Hall* was at Sarnia, Ontario where another firewall was being installed to slow the spread of fire to the crew quarters.

On February 26, 1981, repairmen were working in the stairway leading to the bridge of the *Montcliffe Hall*. Sparks from a welder's torch started a small fire which quickly filled the stairway and the wheelhouse with flames and thick smoke.

Firefighters from Sarnia and Point Edward, Ontario responded immediately and trained their hoses on the burning wheelhouse of the ship. The U. S. Coast Guard ship Bramble, with firefighting equipment at the ready, stood by in the river to assist if needed.

The fire was quickly extinguished but not before the crew quarters and pilothouse were extensively damaged. The navigational and communication equipment of the ship were all destroyed. The ship would require expensive repairs before she could sail again.

The third of the sisters the Hall Corporation Shipping Ltd. purchased, the *Rhine Ore* was renamed the *Steelcliffe Hall*. In 1988 the *Steelcliffe Hall* was sold to N. M. Patterson & Sons Ltd. Marine Division of Thunder Bay, Ontario. The new owners changed her name again to the *Windoc*.

On August 11, 2001 the *Windoc* was in transit up the Welland Canal after having taken on a cargo of 26,000 metric tons of grain in Thunder Bay, Ontario bound for Montreal.

The Welland Canal is an approximately 27 long mile waterway which allows maritime traffic to travel between Lake Erie and Lake Ontario. The canal has eight locks to raise or lower the ships a total of 326.5-feet from the level of Lake Erie down to the level of Lake Ontario. Also crossing the Welland Canal are more than 20 bridges.

The Windoc. *From the collection of Jeff Cameron.*

Anytime there are that many bridges on a busy waterway like the Welland Canal, there are bound to be ship and bridge accidents. The *Windoc* was involved in just such an accident.

Having traveled about 12 miles up the canal, Captain Ken Strong, wheelsman, and the ship's third officer were in the pilothouse as they approached the Allanburg Bridge, bridge #11.

The damaged Windoc *the day after the accident. From the collection of David J. Wobser.*

The Allanburg Bridge is a vertical lift bridge. The entire span rises to permit maritime traffic to pass below. The bridge operators' control room is mounted above the roadbed and rises with the span.

As the *Windoc* approached bridge 11, the men in the pilothouse observed the flashing amber approach light; a series of colored lights had been developed to allow communication between the bridge operator and the vessels passing through it. The amber light indicated that the bridge operator was aware that the vessel was approaching.

The *Windoc* drew closer to the span, a flashing red light was seen as the span was being raised. When the roadbed was up to its full extent, the light changed to solid green. The *Windoc* lined up with the center line of the bridge and proceeded under it.

The *Windoc* was about halfway through the bridge, when the third officer noticed that the bridge span was descending!

Captain Strong quickly sounded several blasts on the ship's whistle and called on the VHF radio to the Traffic Control Center to inform them that the bridge was lowering prematurely.

The *Windoc's* superstructure had not yet cleared the bridge span!

The damage to the stern section of the Windoc. *From the collection of David J. Wobser.*

The Windoc *the day after the accident rests on the bottom after the fire was extinguished. From the collection of David J. Wobser.*

The radio call and the blasting of the ship's whistle had no effect on the bridge, it continued to lower. The ship was unable to stop in time to avoid a collision with the bridge's roadbed.

Seeing a collision was immanent, Captain Strong ordered everyone out of the wheelhouse. All left but wheelsman, Alan Hiscock. He was afraid the ship would drift out of control if he left the wheel, so he laid on the deck of the bridge.

The *Windoc* rammed the Allanburg Bridge at about the level of the wheelhouse; windows smashed inward, the steel of the superstructure ripped with a metallic shriek. Much of the wheelhouse was pushed backward onto the crew quarters. With the ship still powering forward, the smokestack was next to be struck by the bridge. The structural steel and concrete of the bridge gave way in a crunching sound until the stack was torn from the deck. The stack toppled backwards landing on the aft deck.

The starboard anchor of the *Windoc* was released in an attempt to stop the crippled ship. The ship swung around until it came to rest about a half of a mile beyond the bridge, the bow against the east bank and the *Windoc's* stern was embedded in the west bank; effectively blocking the waterway.

Smoke was detected coming from the crew quarters; soon flames were climbing into the sky from the stricken ship. The crew had mustered at the sound of the general alarm and broke out the firefighting equipment. Area firefighters responded quickly to fight the rapidly spreading fire. Streams of water were pumped onto the burning aft section of the *Windoc* from both sides of the canal, finally being extinguished the following day.

The bridge operator claimed that he could see the stern of the *Windoc* passing and that he thought the ship had passed the tower. However, his judgment may have been impaired by the fact that he finished working his regular shift of that day and was working a double shift, or maybe the prescription pain killer he had taken impaired his judgment, or maybe it was the two to four glasses of wine he admitted to drinking at lunch. Or maybe it was a combination of all three that contributed to the bridge operator lowering the bridge before the *Windoc* had fully passed under it.

All three sisters, the *Ems Ore*, the *Ruhr Ore* and the *Rhine Ore* followed an almost identical path. They were built for the ocean, converted and lengthened for use on the Great Lakes and suffered similar fires.

SHIPS AT LEAST 800 FEET
INDIANA HARBOR

In northern Lake Michigan, ships traveling between the Straits of Mackinaw and lower Lake Michigan ports have an option of following different shipping lanes which take the ship down the middle or the east or west side of the lake depending on the final destination. For ships traveling between the Straits of Mackinaw and northern Lake Michigan or Green Bay harbors, a shipping lane has been established which takes the ship across the top of Lake Michigan then down to the ports.

This northern lane takes the ships through a narrow passage, less than five miles wide, between the Lansing Shoals and Squaw Island.

At the south end of the passage is tiny Squaw Island. A half of a mile long and almost the same in width, the island is surrounded by a shallow reef extending north into the lake for almost two miles.

Lansing Shoal at the north of the narrow passage is a reef just over five miles off the mainland of Michigan's Upper Peninsula, with charted depths as low as 26- to 16-feet. The Lansing Shoal Lighthouse stands to warn and guide ships past the treacherous shoal.

In the 1890's, shipping traffic through the passage increased due to iron ore shipments from Escanaba, Michigan at the northern end of Lake

Indiana Harbor   **998 Feet in Length**

The 998-foot long Indiana Harbor *passing under Port Huron's Bluewater Bridge. From the Great Lakes Photographic collections of Dick Wicklund.*

Michigan. Mariners demanded that a lighthouse be built to warn ships of the shoal. For the 1901 shipping season, the Lightship LV55 was anchored in the area to meet the request of mariners for a navigational light.

Lightship LV55 maintained its watch over the shoal until 1920 when her wood hull was found to be rotting and repairs cost prohibitive.

The Lightship LV98 was then assigned to duty at the shallow Lansing Shoal. The 101-foot long ship was on station at Lansing Shoals guiding ships safely by the shallows until 1928 when the Lansing Shoals lighthouse was opened.

The lighthouse is built atop a 20-foot high, 74-foot square concrete foundation. The foundation was heavily reinforced due to the thick ice flows which are common to the area. The lower deck of the building was built to serve as a boat house, galley

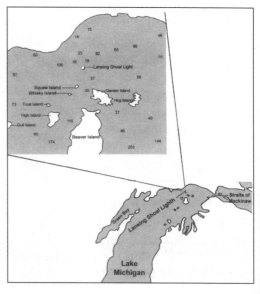

and mess for the crew. Above rose a three story tower, 13-feet at the base and eleven feet square at the top. In the lantern room a third order Fresnel lens showed a beacon that could be seen for 16 miles.

On September 9, 1993 in the early morning hours, the American Steamship Company ship *Indiana Harbor* sailed from Sturgeon Bay, Wisconsin bound for the Straits of Mackinaw. The ship had just completed minor repairs and was heading back into service.

The *Indiana Harbor* was a modern ship having been built in 1979 and equipped with all of the latest technological advances in propulsion, loading and unloading equipment and navigational electronics. The ship was 1,000-feet in length, 105-feet wide and 56-feet in draft allowing the huge ship to carry 78,850 tons of cargo.

While crossing the top of Lake Michigan, the third mate was the duty officer on the bridge, all systems seemed to be functioning and it was recorded that the ship was making way in clear weather. The ship, operating on automatic pilot was traveling eastward towards the Straits of Mackinaw when it came to an abrupt stop as the 1,000-foot ship rammed head on into the Lansing Shoals Lighthouse!

Despite all of the state of the art electronic equipment, the *Indiana Harbor* ran into the stationary lighthouse that had been in the same spot for 65 years. The *Indiana Harbor* received a 50 square foot gash in her bow requiring almost two million dollars in repairs. The lighthouse foundation sustained about one hundred thousand dollars of damage but it continued to function.

After a Coast Guard investigation, it was found that the ship was following the northeast shipping lane towards the Lansing Shoals and would change course near the shoals to the east towards the Straits of Mackinaw. But, the third mate failed to make the course change and the ship simply ran into the lighthouse.

On January 3, 1996 the huge *Indiana Harbor* was once again the subject of another shipping incident. The ship, while maneuvering in the St. Marys

The Lansing Shoals Lighthouse. United States Coast Guard photograph.

The huge Indiana Harbor *departing Duluth, Minnesota. From the Great Lakes Photographic collection of Dick Wicklund.*

River in a "pea-soup" fog wandered out of the West Neebish shipping channel and grounded.

The grounding tore an underwater gash in her port bow with a 40-foot long crease in her hull plates running astern. With the hole in her hull, the ship was taking on water but the flooding was limited to a fore peak tank. The intact bulkheads prevented the flooding from reaching any other sections of the ship. The ship's pumps were running and the *Indiana Harbor* was not in immediate danger of sinking.

The *Indiana Harbor* backed off under her own power and limped to the narrow Rock Cut, blocking the path of any down-bound vessel traffic. The ships waiting to pass through the river had to anchor and await passage. The down-bound ships that

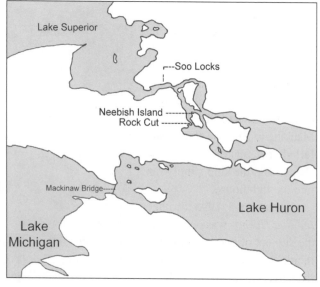

had already locked through anchored below the locks, while others above the locks had to anchor in Lake Superior's Whitefish Bay.

The typical January temperatures produced a rapid freezing of the lake and the river. The *Indiana Harbor* had to be moved soon or the ships at anchor would be trapped by winter's ice. The river had already been filling with flow ice and the Coast Guard had four ice breakers working to maintain the shipping channels and the flow of cargo between the lakes. But, now with a 1,000-foot freighter blocking the down-bound channel, the ice breakers had to keep the river open and free for the freighters as the ice grew thicker.

Indiana Harbor was moved, very slowly, south of Neebish Island where the Coast Guard made a thorough inspection of the damaged ship.

Once the *Indiana Harbor* was removed, the four Coast Guard ice breakers set to work releasing the 13 down-bound freighters and four up-bound ships that had been caught in the ice.

GLOSSARY

Abandon Ship Signal - A long blast on the ship's whistle notifying everyone onboard that the ship is in severe peril and for all to leave the ship by lifeboats or any means immediately.

Aft / After - Towards the rear end of a ship.

Beam - The largest width of a ship.

Barge - A barge is designed or rebuilt as a vessel to be pushed or pulled by another ship. The barge, usually without any means of propulsion, transports cargo on the Great Lakes and its harbors and tributaries.

Bilge - Lowest part of the interior of a ship's hull.

Bit - A wood or metal structural post on a tugboat to which the towline is attached.

Boiler - A metal container where water is heated to create steam to power the steam engines.

Bollard - A post or cast metal device on a dock or wharf. The mooring lines of a ship are secured to it to hold the ship to the dock or wharf.

Bow - The front end of a ship. The port bow, starboard bow refers to the left and right of the forward sides of the vessel.

Breakers - The waves crashing on the shore or rocks.

Bridge - The pilothouse or wheelhouse. The location on the ship where the ship is steered.

Capsize - When a ship turns over; rolls over to the port or starboard.

Checking Speed - To reduce speed.

Chief Engineer - The crew member who is in charge of the engine and machinery of the ship.

Companionway, Passageway - A passage, corridor, or hallway on a ship.

Davits - The brackets which hold lifeboats on the ship and are used to raise or lower the lifeboats.

Deadlights - Portholes

Deck Cargo - Cargo transported on the deck of a ship rather than in the hold below deck.

Distress signal - A signal used to alert others of a disaster at sea and call for assistance.

Drydock - An area where a ship sails in and the water is pumped out. The drydock allows repairs to be made to the hull below the water line.

Firebox - The chamber in which a fire is built to heat the water in the boiler on a steam powered ship.

First Mate - Second in command of the ship behind the captain. To be a mate, the person must meet federal licensing requirements.

Fog Signal - A steam or compressed air powered whistle sounded in times of reduced visibility to notify other ships.

Fore - The forward or front of the ship.

Foredeck - A deck towards the bow of a ship.

Founder - To sink.

Freeboard - The part of a ship's hull above the surface of the water.

Freshening - The wind increasing; the wind is freshening.

Full Ahead - A ship moving at top speed in a forward direction.

Gale Force Wind - A strong wind from 32 to 63 miles per hour.

Gangway - A passageway in a side of a ship where passengers and cargo enter and depart the vessel.

Glass or Glasses - A telescope or binoculars.

Harbor of Refuge - A harbor, natural or man made, designed for ships to seek refuge in times of severe weather.

Hawser - A large rope used to tow or secure a ship.

Hold - An area on a ship below the deck where cargo is stowed.

Holed - A hull of a ship being punctured in a collision or by striking an object.

Hull - The body of the vessel.

Jacob's ladder - A rope ladder.

Keel - A large wood or steel beam running bow to stern at the lowest point of the ship. It forms the backbone of the ship.

Knot - Speed of a ship which equals one nautical mile per hour.

Lee - Protection; the side of a ship protected from the wind.

Lifeboat station - The location of a lifeboat on a ship.

Life jackets, Life preserver - a personal floatation device used to support an individual at the surface of the water.

GLOSSARY

Lightened - Intentionally reducing the weight of the ship.

Lines - Ropes used on a ship.

List - When a ship leans to port or starboard, left or right, due to unevenly stored cargo or from taking on water.

Lumber Hooker - A ship involved with the transportation of wood products.

Mid ship - In the middle of the ship from the bow to the stern.

Mooring Lines - Lines used to secure a vessel to a dock, pier or wharf.

Passenger Ship - A ship designed to transport passengers on journeys extending more than just a few hours.

Range Lights - Lighted beacons spaced a distance from one another. A ship is on course when entering a river or harbor when it positions itself so the lights are aligned above one another.

Pilothouse - The Bridge of a ship; where the ship is controlled, steered, and navigated.

Pitch - The forward and aft rocking of a ship.

Port - The left side of a boat when looking towards the front.

Prow - The forward part of a vessel.

Radar - A device which sends out a strong beam of radio waves. When it strikes an object it reflects back. The radar can then determine the distance away, direction of movement and speed of the object.

Reef - A rocky or sandy feature at or near the surface of the water.

Roll - The sideward, port to starboard, movement of a ship.

Schooner - A sailing craft having two masts, one fore, the other aft.

Shipping lane - Areas of a lake which ships must be traveling in a specific direction; up bound or down bound lanes.

Shoal Water - Shallow water.

Slow astern - A ship operating at slow speed in a backward direction.

Soo Locks - Situated between Lakes Superior and Huron the locks raise ships 22-feet to the higher level of Lake Superior, or lower downbound ships to the Lake Huron level.

Starboard - The right side of a boat when looking towards the bow.

Stern - The aft or rear of a boat.

Swing Bridge - A bridge which rotates from a central position. The bridge remains open for ship traffic to pass and closes only when it is needed. It is usually used for railroad bridges.

Tanker - A vessel specifically designed to transport liquid cargo, such as gasoline or other forms of oil.

Telegraph - A mechanical devise used to transmit instructions to and from the bridge of a ship to the engine room.

Tender - A small boat which carries crew, passengers and supplies between a ship or lighthouse and shore.

Tug - The workhorse of the lakes. Tugs have been used to assist other ships to docks, or through congested waterways, tow barges, to transport cargo and passengers, for fishing, ice breaking, as a wrecking vessel and as a rescue vessel.

Turned Turtle - A common phrase to describe a ship which has been capsized and its bottom is above the surface.

Wharf - A structure built along a waterway where ships can tie up and discharge or take on cargo or passengers.

Wheelsman/Helmsman - The person who met the licensing restriction to be qualified to steer the ship.

Yawl - A small boat on a ship used by the crew to get to shore from an anchorage.

BIBLIOGRAPHY

Ships At Least 400-Feet In Length

William C. Warren

Presque Isle County Advisor, Rogers City, Michigan, November 13, 20, 1947, December 3, 1947, February 30, 1948.

The Alpena News, Alpena Michigan, November 10, 1947.

Doner, Mary Francis, *The Salvager; The life of Captain Tom Reid on the Great Lakes*, Ross and Haines Inc., Minneapolis, Mn, 1959.

James Gayley

Maritime History of the Great Lakes, http://www.hhpl.on.ca/greatlakes/wrecks/details.asp?ID=7511.

Swayze, David, D., "Shipwreck! A Comprehensive Directory of Over 3,700 Shipwrecks on the Great Lakes.", Harbor House Publishing, Inc., Boyne City, Michigan, 1992.

The Daily Mining Gazette, Houghton and Calumet, Michigan, August 8, 9, 1912.

The Evening News, Sault Ste. Marie, Michigan, August 8, 1912.

The Great Lakes Shipwreck file: Total losses of Great Lakes Ships 1679-1999, Swayze, David, D., http://www.boatnerd.com/swayze/shipwreck/.

Cyprus

The Evening News, Sault Ste. Marie, Michigan October 12, 1907.

Swayze, David, D., "Shipwreck! A Comprehensive Directory of Over 3,700 Shipwrecks on the Great Lakes.", Harbor House Publishing, Inc., Boyne City, Michigan, 1992.

Shanks, Ralph and Wick York, "The U.S. Life Saving Service: Heroes, Rescues and Architecture of the Early Coast Guard." Costano Books, Petaluma, California, 2000.

McGrath, Captain Ray, I., "Great Lakes Stories; Ashore after 50 years" Border Enterprises, Sault Saint Marie, Michigan, 1996.

Ratigan, William, "Great Lakes Shipwrecks and Survivors" Galahad Books, New York, New York, 1960.

Boyer, Dwight, "Great Stories of the Great Lakes and Thrilling tales of Tragedy, humor and Heroism" Dodd, Mead and Company, New York, New York. 1966.

Stonehouse, Frederick, "Wreck Ashore; U.S. Life-Saving Service Legendary Heroes of the Great lakes" Lake Superior Port Cities, Duluth, Minnesota. 1994.

Henry Steinbrenner

Http://www.pasty.com/~barbspage/steinbrenner.html.

Marquette Mining Journal, Marquette, Michigan, May 11, 12, 13, 1953.

The Daily Mining Gazette, Houghton, Michigan, May, 11, 12, 13, 1953.

The Evening News, Sault Ste. Marie, Michigan, May, 11, 12, 13, 15, 1953.

United States Coast Guard Accident Report, Washington D.C., July 10, 1954, *Henry Steinbrenner*-a-9 Bd.

The Ships of November 1913

Deedler, William, R., "Hell Hath' No Fury Like a Great Lakes Fall Storm; Great Lakes White Hurricane November 1913." http://www.crh.noaa.gov/dtx/stm_1913.htm.

Doner, Mary Francis, "The Salvager, The life of Captain Tom Reid on the Great Lakes." Ross and Haines Inc., Minneapolis, Minnesota, 1958.

Historical Collection of the Great Lakes, Bowling Green State University.

Swayze, David D., "Shipwreck!", Harbor House Publishers, Inc., Boyne City, Michigan, 1992.

The New York Times, New York, New York, November 13, 1913.

The Daily Review, Decatur, Illinois, November 14, 1913.

E. M. Ford

The Scanner, The Toronto Marine Historical Society. http://www.hhpl.on.ca/GreatLakes/Documents/Scanner/07/08/defaults.as.

E.M. Ford, Presque Isle. By Brian Ferguson, http://www.boatnerd.com/pictures/fleet/emford.htm.

Milwaukee Sentinel, Milwaukee, Wisconsin, December 26, 1979.

Inland Seas, Volume 55, Number 2, 1999, The E.M. Ford, Patrick Lapinski.

Swayze, David D., "Shipwreck!", Harbor House Publishers, Inc., Boyne City, Michigan, 1992.

The Evening News, Sault Saint Marie, Michigan, December 26, 1979.

The Alpena News, Alpena, Michigan, December 26, 27, 1979.

M/V *Montrose*

The Detroit News, Detroit, Michigan July 31, 1962.

The Detroit News, Detroit, Michigan, August 1, 1962.

The Detroit News Rearview Mirror, "The night the *Montrose* sank in the Detroit River."
http://info.detnews,com/history/story/index.cfm?id=164&category-events.

The Lightship. Newsletter of the Lake Huron Lore Marine Society, Bluewater Area Shiipwrecks; *Montrose*, by Skip Gillham.Volume XXVIII. No. 1.

The Times Herald, Port Huron, Michigan, July 31, 1962.

City of Bangor

Daily Mining Gazette, Houghton-Calumet, Michigan, December 1, 2, 4, 7, 8, 9, 1926.

Historical Collection of the Great Lakes, Bowling Green State University.

Swayze, David D., "Shipwreck!", Harbor House Publishers, Inc., Boyne City, Michigan, 1992.

Sunday Mining Gazette, Houghton-Calumet, Michigan, December 5, 1926.

Marquette Mining Journal, Marquette, Michigan, December 3, 4, 7, 1926.

Penobscot

Buffalo Evening News, Buffalo, New York, October 30, 31, 1951.

Chicago Daily Tribune, Chicago, Illinois, October 30, 1951.

Detroit News, Detroit, Michigan, October 30, 1951.

Historical Collection of the Great Lakes, Bowling Green State University.

Swayze, David D., "Shipwreck!", Harbor House Publishers, Inc., Boyne City, Michigan, 1992.

United States Coast Guard Accident Report, 27, March, 1952.

James H. Reed and the *Frank E. Vigor*

Detroit Free Press, Detroit, Michigan, April 27, 28, 1944.

Detroit News, Detroit, Michigan April 27, 1944.

Detroit Times, Detroit, Michigan, April 27, 28, 1944.

Dunnville Chronicle, Dunnville, Ohio.

Shipwrecks of the Great Lakes, by Skip Gillham.

Swayze, David, D., "Shipwreck! A Comprehensive Directory of Over 3,700 Shipwrecks on the Great Lakes.", Harbor House Publishing, Inc., Boyne City, Michigan, 1992.

The *Sidney E. Smith*

Historical Collection of the Great Lakes, Bowling Green State University.

Swayze, David D., "Shipwreck!", Harbor House Publishers, Inc., Boyne City, Michigan, 1992.

The Times Herald, Port Huron, Michigan, September 24, 1962.

The Times Herald, Port Huron, Michigan, June 5, 1972.

Ships At Least 500-Feet In Length

S.S. Pioneer

Marine Board of Investigation: *S.S. Pioneer-M/V Wallschiff*, January 7, 1954, United States Coast Guard.

Port Huron Times Herald, Port Huron, Michigan. October 3, 4, 5, 1953.

J.F. Schoellkopf Jr.

Houghton Historical Society, Upper Peninsula Digitization Center Collection.

http://michiganhighways.org/indepth/zilwaukee.html, the Zilwaukee Bridge.

Michigan Department of Transportation, http://www.michigan.gov/mdot/0.1607,7151-9620_11154-11188-28585-,00.html.

The history of the three bridges to span the canal between Houghton and Hancock, Kevin E. Musser, HYPERLINK "http://www.copperrange.org/" The Copper Range Railroad and Copper Country Historical Homepage.

Swayze, David D., "Shipwreck!", Harbor House Publishers, Inc., Boyne City, Michigan, 1992.

BIBLIOGRAPHY

J. P. Morgan Jr.

Daily Mining Gazette, Houghton, Michigan, June 24, 1948.

Decision and final order of the Commandant United States Coast Guard. In the matter of license No. 42207 issued to Frank W. Quinn., J. F. Farley, Admiral, United States Coast Guard. November 15, 1949.

The Evening News, Sault Ste. Marie, Michigan, June 24, 1948.

Swayze, David D., "Shipwreck! A Comprehenshive Directory of over 3,700 Shipwrecks on the Great Lakes." Harbor House Publishing, Boyne City, Michigan, 1992.

William C. Moreland

Doner, Mary Francis, "The Salvager, The life of Captain Tom Reid on the Great Lakes." Ross and Haines Inc., Minneapolis, Minnesota, 958.

Inland Seas, Volume 5.2, 1949.

Marquette Mining Journal, Marquette Michigan, October 20, 21, 1910.

Swartz, David D., "Shipwreck!", Harbor House Publications, Boyne City, Michigan, 1992.

The *W.C. Moreland*, http://filias.net/narcosis/sawtooth.htm.

The Scanner, Monthly News Bulletin of the Toronto Marine Historical Society, Ship of the month *No. 4 Parkdale*, http://www.hhpl.on.ca/Great.

Lakes/Documents/Scanner/02/03/default.asp?ID=c004, http://www.hhpl.on.ca/Great .

Lakes/Documents/Scanner/02/03/default.asp?ID=c007

William C. Moreland, http://www.shipwrecks.net/shipwrecks/keweenaw/moreland.html.

George M. Humphrey

Inland Seas, Volume 1, January 1995, "Recovery of the Steamer *Humphrey*, Jewell R. Dean.

Swayze, David D., "Shipwreck!", Harbor House Publishers, Inc., Boyne City, Michigan, 1992

The Evening News, Sault Ste. Marie, Michigan, June 15, 16, 1943.

Time Magazine, "Mackinaw Miracle," October 02, 1944.

Daniel J. Morrell

Department of Transportation, Marine Board of Investigation, Marine Board of Investigation, *S.S. Daniel J. Morrell*, Sinking with loss of life, Lake Huron, 29, November 1966. Released March 4, 1968.

Hale, Dennis, Presentations by Mr. Hale. Dennis Hale, P.O. Box 104, Rock Creek, OH 44084. Authors note: If you need a Great Lakes speaker, Mr. Hale does a Fantastic job.

Hale, Dennis, Juhl, Tim, Pat and Jim Stayer. Sole Survivor: Dennis Hale's Own Story. Lakeshore Charters & Marine Exploration, Inc. Lexington, Michigan. 1996.

Harbor Beach Times, Harbor Beach, Michigan, December 8, 15, 1966.

Http://web1.msue.msu.edu/iosco/nordmeer.htm.

National Transportation Board, Marine Accident Report, Released 4, March, 1968.

The Alpena News, Alpena, Michigan, November 21, 22, 29, 30, 1966.

The Bay City Times, Bay City, Michigan, November 28, December 1, 2, 3, 1966.

The Evening News, Sault Ste. Marie, November 29, 30, December 1, 2, 3, 5, 1966.

The Columbus Dispatch, Columbus, Ohio, Bernard Rogers McCoy, November 26, 2006.

The Times Herald, Port Huron, Michigan, Danielle Quisenberry, "*Morrell's* horror lingers four decades after sinking" November 2006.

Cedarville

Marine Board of Investigation, *Cedarville-Topdalsfjord*, A-9 Bd, 6 February, 1967.

Wreck of the *Cedarville*, http://www.msue.msu.edu/iosco/cedarville.htm.

The Evening News, Sault Ste. Marie, Michigan, May 7, 8,10, 11, 12, 1965.

The Alpena News, Alpena, Michigan, May 7, 8, 10, 11, 12, 13, 14, 1965.

The Presque Isle County Advance, Rogers City, Michigan, May 13, 20, 1965.

BIBLIOGRAPHY

Ships At Least 600-Feet In Length

Donnacona

Special Thanks to Al Hart for opening his archives and helping with research on the *Donnacona*.

The Detroit News, Detroit, Michigan, December 16, 17, 1964.

Detroit Free Press, Detroit, Michigan, December 17, 18, 1964.

The Times Herald, Port Huron, Michigan, December 17, 1964.

Frontenac

http://www.rudyalicelighthouse.net/Erielts/Buffalo/buffalo.html.

The Marquette Mining Journal, Marquette, Michigan, November 23, 1979.

Swayze, David D., "Shipwreck: A comprehensive Directory of over 3,700 Shipwrecks on the Great Lakes", Harbor House Publications, Boyne City, Michigan, 1992.

Telescope, Great Lakes Maritime Institute, Detroit Michigan,November-December 2001.

The Evening News, Sault Ste. Marie, Michigan, November 23, 1979.

The Daily Mining Gazette, Houghton, Michigan, November 23, 1979.

S.S. Elton Hoyt II and the *S.S. Enders M. Voorhees*

The Port Huron Tomes Herald, Port Huron, Michigan, November 25, 1950.

The United States Coast Guard Marine Board of Investigation Report, *Elton Hoyt II - Enders M. Voorhees* C-9 Bd, March 2, 1951.

Swayze, David D., "Shipwreck: A comprehensive Directory of over 3,700 Shipwrecks on the Great Lakes", Harbor House Publications, Boyne City, Michigan, 1992.

Buffalo

Bay City Times, Bay City, Michigan, September 17, 18, 19, 20, 21.22, 24, 1990.

National Transportation Safety Board Marine Accident Report. Fire and explosion aboard the U.S. Tankership Jupiter, NTSB/MAR-91/04, PB 91-916404.

BoatNerd.com, http://lighthouse.boatnerd.com/gallery/Detroit/Detroitriverlight.html.

Detroit News, Detroit, Michigan, December 12, 1997.

Carl D. Bradley

United States Coast Guard Marine Board of Investigation report; Foundering of the S.S. Carl D. Bradley, Lake Michigan, 18 November 1958.

Caesar, Pete, Lake Michigan Wrecks VI, Great Lakes Marine Research, Green Bay, Wisconsin, 1996.

Mariners Weather Log, Vol. 48, No. 3, National Oceanographic Administration, Skip Gilham, December 2004.

Manistique Pioneer Tribune, August 24, 1995, Marilyn S. Fischer.

http://www.mssd.org/publications/glswr/bradley.htm, Carl D. Bradley by Keith E. Smith.

The Evening News, Sault Ste. Marie, Michigan, November 20, 1958.

Presque Isle County Advance, Rogers City, Michigan, November 20, 27, 1958.

Time Archive, December 1, 1958, The Death of the Bradley, http://www.time.com/printout/0,8816,891981,00.html.

The Mate's Radio Call, By James Donahue, http://perduabo10.tripod.com/ships/id135.html.

Swayze, David D., "Shipwreck! A Comprehensive Directory of over 3,700 Shipwrecks on the Great Lakes." Harbor House Publishing, Boyne City, Michigan, 1992.

Ships At Least 700-Feet In Length

Edmund Fitzgerald

Department of Transportation Coast Guard Marine Casualty Report. S.S. Edmund Fitzgerald; sinking in Lake Superior on November 10, 1975 with loss of life. U.S. Coast Guard Marine Board of Investigation report and Commandant's Action, Report No. USCG 16732/64216.

Detroit Free Press, Detroit, Michigan, November 11, 12, 1975.

Detroit News, Detroit, Michigan, November 11, 12, 13, 1975.

National Transportation Safety Board, Washington, D.C. 20594, Marine Accident Report S.S. Edmund Fitzgerald sinking in Lake Superior, November 10, 1975, Report Number: NTSB-Mar-78-3.

"Significant Events in the History of the Edmund Fitzgerald", Compiled by

BIBLIOGRAPHY

Tony Wesley. http://tonywesley.com/edm-fritz.html.

Stonehouse, Frederick, "The Wreck of the *Edmund Fitzgerald*", Avery Color Studios, Inc. Qwinn, Michigan, 2006.

Swayze, David D., "Shipwreck! A Comprehenshive Directory of over 3,700 Shipwrecks on the Great Lakes." Harbor House Publishing, Boyne City, Michigan, 1992.

Telescope, 40th Anniversary Launch of the *S.S. Edmund Fitzgerald*; $8 Million Dollar~7500 Ton Laker is Born, May- August, 1998, Volume XLVI; Number 2.

The Evening News, Sault Ste. Marie, Michigan, November 11, 12, 13,14,15, 1975.

The Sinking of the *S.S. Edmund Fitzgerald*-November 10, 1975, http://cimss.ssec.wisc.edu/wxwise/fitz.html.

Montcilffe Hall - Cartiercliffe Hall - Steelcliffe Hall

http://www.boatnerd.com/windoc/, *Windoc* Accident August 11, 2001.

http:www.wellandcanal.ca/transit/2001/august/windocstory.html, *Windoc* & Bridge 11 collision-August 11, 2001.

http://www.wellandcanal.com/mishap.html, *Windoc* hit by Allanburg lift-bridge.

Swayze, David D., "Shipwreck: A comprehensive Directory of over 3,700 Shipwrecks on the Great Lakes", Harbor House Publications, Boyne City, Michigan, 1992.

Telescope, Great Lakes Maritime Institute, Detroit Michigan,November-December 2001.

The Evening News, Sault Ste. Marie, Michigan, June 5, 6, 1979.

The Daily Mining Gazette, Houghton, Michigan, June 5, 6, 7, 8, 1979.

The Times Herald, Port Huron, Michigan, February 27, 1981.

Transportation Safety Board of Canada, Marine Reflextions Magazine, Issue 22, July 2005. http: ww.tsb.gc.ca/en/publications/reflexions/marine/2005/issue_22 marine_issue22

Grosse Ile Toll Bridge

Detroit Free Press, Detroit, Michigan, September 7, 1992.

The Detroit News, Detroit, Michigan, August 7, 1965.

The Port Huron, Port Huron, Michigan, August 7, 1965.

United States Court of Appeals, Sixth Circuit, Grosse Ile Bridge Company vs. American Steamship Company. September 7, 2002.

The Grosse Ile Bridge Company,
http://gibc.typepad.com/toll_bridge_facts/about/index.html.

Ships At Least 800-Feet In Length

Indiana Harbor

Seeing the Light; Lighthouse of the Western Great Lakes, Lansing Shoal Light, Terry Pepper, http://www.terrypepper.com/lights.

Duluth Shipping News, http://www.duluthshippingnews.com.

BoatNerd.com, http://www.boatnerd.com.

The Evening News, Sault Ste. Marie, Michigan, January 4, 5, 6, 1996.

ACKNOWLEDGEMENTS

No historical endeavor can be accomplished without the assistance and aid of many. I want to thank all of those who contributed.

Bayliss Public Library, and Susan James for assistance with research and access to their photographic collection.

Boatnerd.com the people who respond to my questions: Brian from Buffalo, Brent from Cheboygan, Charlie from The Soo, Chris from Portage, Dave from Florida, Capt R. Metz from Florida, R. Martens from Niagara, Kent from Candiac, QC.

Bowling Green State University, Historical Collections of the Great Lakes, Bowling Green State University. Robert Graham, Archivist.

Buffalo and Erie County Public Library.

Clark, Hugh for his assistance in Canadian geography, access to his photographic collection and for being a friend.

DeFrain, Leonard, The Harbor Beach Historian.

Door County Maritime Museum and Lighthouse Preservation Society, Sturgeon Bay, Wisconsin, June Larson, Assistant Curator.

Gerow, Ed, for sharing his vast knowledge of the Great Lakes and ships.

Grosse Ile Bridge Company, http: //gibc.typepad.com/toll_bridge_facts/about/index.html.

Grosse Ile Historical Society, Clare Koester.

Harbor Beach Public Library, Harbor Beach, Michigan. Vicki Mazure, Director.

Hart, Al for sharing his wealth of archival information about the Great Lakes.

Huskins, David for access to his personal collections.

Kimble, Jan, Historian of the Presque Isle Lighthouse.

Klebba, Ron, Harbor Beach, Michigan for his friendship, knowledge of sailing and boat construction.

Lewis, William D., for access to his personal photograph collection.

Library of Michigan and the State of Michigan Archives, Lansing, Michigan.

Lower Lakes Marine Historical Society, Buffalo, New York.

McGreevy, Robert, A special thank you to Marine Artist Robert McGreevy for allowing the use of some of his paintings on this book. http://mcgreevy.com.

Main, Tom and Linda, Caseville, Michigan for their assistance in sailing terminology, and technique and for sharing their knowledge of the Great Lakes.

Martin, Jeff and Maureen, For use of their Jupiter photographs.

Mehringer, Tom, for sharing his knowledge of the Lakes and S.C.U.B.A. diving experiences.

Milwaukee Public Library, Suzette Lopez of the Great Lake Collection.

Morden, Charlie, thanks for the use of his historical information.

Pepper, Terry, *Seeing the Light,* www.terrypepper.com/lights.

Port Huron Museum. Special thanks to Suzette Bromley, Curator of Collections, Port Huron Michigan, for her assistance.

Presque Isle Lighthouse.

St. Clair Public Library, Port Huron, Michigan.

The Grice House Museum, Harbor Beach, Michigan.

Toledo Lucas County Library, James Marshall, Director.

Unbehaun, Charlie, for his knowledge of diving and sharing information on wrecks.

United States Coast Guard, Historian's Office, Christopher B. Havern, Historian.

University of Wisconsin-Superior, JDH Library, Laura Jacobs.

Voelker, Chuck, for access to his photographic collection.

Whipple, Kerry, thanks for providing information and photographs of the *Cedarville.*

ACKNOWLEDGEMENTS

Williamson, K. Don, for his knowledge of Great Lakes boating.

Wobser, David J., thanks for providing *Windoc* photographs.

Wicklund, Dick, Lake Lore Marine Society, for access to his personal photographic collection.

Wisconsin Maritime Historical Society, Catherine Sanders, Milwaukee, Wisconsin.

ABOUT THE AUTHOR

Geography has played an important part in shaping Wayne "Skip" Kadar's love of the Great Lakes. Throughout his life he has lived in the downriver area of Detroit, Marquette, Harbor Beach and at the family cottage in Manistique, Michigan. Growing and living in these rich historic maritime areas has instilled in him a love of the Great Lakes and their maritime past.

This love has taken him in many directions. He is a certified S.C.U.B.A. diver and avid boater, having owned most all types of boats

Photo by Karen Kadar

from Personal Water Craft to sailboats to a small cruiser. He is involved in lighthouse restoration, serving as the Vice President of the Harbor Beach Lighthouse Preservation Society.

Mr. Kadar enjoys studying and researching Great Lakes maritime history and has made presentations on maritime history on a local, state and international level.

An educator for thirty years, Mr. Kadar retired after 15 years as a high school principal.

Skip lives in Harbor Beach, Michigan with his wife Karen. During the summer Skip can usually be found at the Harbor Beach Marina, on the family boat "Pirate's Lady" or at the lighthouse.

Other Wayne Kadar Titles
By Avery Color Studio:

Great Lakes Passenger Ship Disasters

Great Lakes Freighter, Tanker & Tugboat Disasters

Strange & Unusual Shipwrecks on the Great Lakes

Avery Color Studios, Inc. has a full line of Great Lakes oriented books, puzzles, cookbooks, shipwreck and lighthouse maps, lighthouse posters and Fresnel lens models.

For a free full-color catalog, call **1-800-722-9925**

Avery Color Studios, Inc. products are
available at gift shops and bookstores
throughout the Great Lakes region.